# JONAH, AMOS & HOSEA

*The Faithfulness of God*

John MacArthur

Harper*Christian*
Resources

MacArthur Bible Studies
Jonah, Amos, and Hosea: The Faithfulness of God
© 2023 by John MacArthur

Published in Grand Rapids, Michigan, by HarperChristian Resources. HarperChristian Resources
is a registered trademark of HarperCollins Christian Publishing, Inc.

Requests for information should be sent to customercare@harpercollins.com.

ISBN 978-0-310-12386-6 (softcover)
ISBN 978-0-310-12387-3 (ebook)

HarperChristian Resources titles may be purchased in bulk for church, business, fundraising,
or ministry use. For information, please e-mail ResourceSpecialist@ChurchSource.com.

"Unleashing God's Truth, One Verse at a Time ®" is a trademark of Grace to You. All rights reserved.

Some material from the Introduction, "Keys to the Text," and "Exploring the Meaning" sections are taken
from The MacArthur Bible Commentary, John MacArthur. Copyright © 2005 Thomas Nelson Publishers.

First Printing October 2024 / Printed in the United States of America
23 24 25 26 27 LBC 5 4 3 2 1

# CONTENTS

# INTRODUCTION

One man hears a word from the Lord instructing him to preach a warning of impending judgment to a city packed with wickedness—and then disobeys that word from the Lord by booking passage in the opposite direction. Another man is instructed by the Lord to take a wife and build a family—only to feel the pain of adultery reflected outward from his home to an entire nation. A third man, an unknown shepherd and farmer from a tiny village, is called by God to trek across miles to confront the most powerful members of a neighboring nation.

All of these are the exploits of *prophets* in the Bible—servants of God who were called to speak and act as His spokespersons to nations and individuals who were often uninterested in anything they had to say. As we shall see in this study, the lives of these prophets were often fraught with difficulty. They were largely unpopular, and their lives were frequently in danger. They carried the weight of God's will on their shoulders and the fire of His words on their lips.

This study will focus specifically on the prophets Jonah, Amos, and Hosea. These are three of what are deemed as "Minor Prophets"—so called not because of their relative importance in history but because of the relative brevity of their written records. Although each of these men ministered in different ways, their books hammer home the same critical theme: the faithlessness of humanity in contrast with the unending faithfulness of God.

## THE BOOK OF JONAH
Following the lead of the Hebrew Masoretic text, the title of the book is derived from the principal character, a man named Jonah (meaning "dove"), the son of

Amittai (see Jonah 1:1). Both the Septuagint (LXX) and the Latin Vulgate ascribe the same name.

## Author and Date

The book makes no direct claim regarding authorship. Jonah is repeatedly referred to in the third person, causing some to search for another author; however, it was not an uncommon Old Testament practice for authors to write in the third person (see Exodus 11:3; 1 Samuel 12:11). Furthermore, the autobiographical information revealed within its pages clearly points to Jonah as the author. The firsthand accounts of such unusual events and experiences would be best recounted from the hand of Jonah himself. Nor should the introductory verse suggest otherwise, since prophets such as Hosea, Joel, Micah, Zephaniah, Haggai, and Zechariah have similar openings. According to 2 Kings 14:25, Jonah came from Gath-hepher near Nazareth. The context places him during the long and prosperous reign of Jeroboam II (c. 793–753 BC), making him a prophet to the northern tribes just prior to Amos during the first half of the eighth century BC (c. 760 BC). An unverifiable Jewish tradition says Jonah was the son of the widow of Zarephath whom Elijah raised from the dead (see 1 Kings 17:8–24).

## Background and Setting

As a prophet to the ten northern tribes of Israel, Jonah shares a background and setting with the prophet Amos. The nation was enjoying a time of relative peace and prosperity. Both Syria and Assyria were weak, which allowed Jeroboam II to enlarge the northern borders of Israel to where they had been in the days of David and Solomon (see 2 Kings 14:23–27). Spiritually, however, it was a time of poverty for the ten northern tribes; religion was ritualistic and increasingly idolatrous, and justice had become perverted. Peacetime and wealth had made her bankrupt spiritually, morally, and ethically (see 2 Kings 14:24; Amos 4:1ff.; 5:10–13). As a result, God was about to punish her by bringing destruction and captivity from the Assyrians in 722 BC. Nineveh's repentance may have been aided by the first of two plagues (765 and 759 BC) and a solar eclipse (763 BC), preparing them for Jonah's message of judgment.

## Historical and Theological Themes

Jonah, even though he was a prophet of Israel, is not remembered for his ministry in Israel. This could explain why the Pharisees erringly claimed in Jesus' day that "no prophet has arisen out of Galilee" (John 7:52), even though Jonah was a Galilean. Rather, the book relates the account of Jonah's call to preach repentance to Nineveh and his refusal to go. Nineveh, the capital of Assyria, was infamous for its cruelty and was a historical nemesis of Israel and Judah.

The focus of the book is on that Gentile city, which was founded by Nimrod, the great-grandson of Noah (see Genesis 10:6–12). Perhaps the largest city in the ancient world (see Jonah 1:2; 3:2–3; 4:11), it was nevertheless destroyed about 150 years after the repentance of the generation in the time of Jonah's visit (612 BC), as Nahum prophesied (see Nahum 1:1ff.). Israel's political distaste for Assyria, coupled with a sense of spiritual superiority as the recipient of God's covenant blessing, produced a recalcitrant attitude in Jonah toward God's request for missionary service. Jonah was sent to Nineveh, in part, to shame Israel by the fact that a pagan city had repented at the preaching of a stranger, whereas Israel would not repent even though she had been preached to by many prophets. Jonah was soon to learn that God's love and mercy extends to all of His creatures (see Jonah 4:2, 10–11), not just His covenant people (see Genesis 9:27; 12:3; Leviticus 19:33–34; 1 Samuel 2:10; Isaiah 2:2; Joel 2:28–32).

The book of Jonah reveals God's sovereign rule over mankind and all creation. Creation came into being through Him (see Jonah 1:9) and responds to His every command (see 1:4, 17; 2:10; 4:6–7; see also Mark 4:41). Jesus used the repentance of the Ninevites to rebuke the Pharisees, thereby illustrating the hardness of the Pharisees' hearts and their unwillingness to repent (see Matthew 12:38–41; Luke 11:29–32). The heathen city of Nineveh repented at the preaching of a reluctant prophet, but the Pharisees would not repent at the preaching of the greatest of all prophets, in spite of overwhelming evidence that He was their Lord and Messiah.

Jonah is a picture of Israel, who was chosen and commissioned by God to be His witness to the world (see Isaiah 43:10–12; 44:8), who rebelled against His will (see Exodus 32:1–4; Judges 2:11–19; Ezekiel 6:1–5; Mark 7:6–9), but who has been miraculously preserved by God through centuries of exile and dispersion to finally preach His truth (see Jeremiah 30:11; 31:35–37; Hosea 3:3–5; Revelation 7:1–8; 14:1–3).

## INTERPRETIVE CHALLENGES

The primary challenge is whether the book is to be interpreted as historical narrative or as allegory/parable. The grand scale of the miracles, such as being kept alive three days and nights in a big fish, has led some skeptics and critics to deny their historical validity and substitute spiritual lessons, either to the constituent parts (allegory) or to the book as a whole (parable). But however grandiose and miraculous the events may have been, the narrative must be viewed as historical. Centered on a historically identifiable Old Testament prophet who lived in the eighth century BC, the account has been recorded in narrative form; there is no alternative but to understand Jonah as historical. Furthermore, Jesus did not teach the story of Jonah as a parable but as an actual account firmly rooted in history (see Matthew 12:38–41; 16:4; Luke 11:29–32).

# THE BOOK OF AMOS

As with each of the Minor Prophets, the title comes from the name of the prophet to whom God gave His message (see Amos 1:1). Amos's name means "burden" or "burden-bearer." He is not to be confused with Amoz ("stout, strong"), the father of Isaiah (see Isaiah 1:1).

## AUTHOR AND DATE

Amos was from Tekoa, a small village ten miles south of Jerusalem. He is the only prophet to give his occupation before declaring his divine commission. He was not of priestly or noble descent but worked as a "sheepbreeder" (Amos 1:1; see also 2 Kings 3:4) and a "tender of sycamore fruit" (Amos 7:14). He was a contemporary of Jonah (see 2 Kings 14:25), Hosea (see Hosea 1:1), and Isaiah (see Isaiah 1:1). The date of writing is mid-eighth century BC, during the reigns of Uzziah, king of Judah (c. 790–739 BC) and Jeroboam II, king of Israel (c. 793–753 BC), two years before a memorable earthquake (see Amos 1:1; Zechariah 14:5).

## BACKGROUND AND SETTING

Amos was a Judean prophet called to deliver a message primarily to the northern tribes of Israel (see Amos 7:15). Politically, it was a time of prosperity under the long and secure reign of Jeroboam II who, following the example of his father Joash (see 2 Kings 13:25), significantly "restored the territory of Israel" (2 Kings 14:25). It was also a time of peace with both Judah (see Amos 5:4–5) and her more distant neighbors; the ever-present menace of Assyria was subdued, possibly because of Nineveh's repentance at the preaching of Jonah (see Jonah 3:10). Spiritually, however, it was a time of rampant corruption and moral decay (see Amos 4:1; 5:10–13; 2 Kings 14:24).

## HISTORICAL AND THEOLOGICAL THEMES

Amos addresses Israel's two primary sins: (1) an absence of true worship, and (2) a lack of justice. In the midst of their ritualistic performance of worship, they were not pursuing the Lord with their hearts (see 4:4–5; 5:4–6) nor following His standard of justice with their neighbors (see 5:10–13; 6:12). This apostasy, evidenced by continual, willful rejection of the prophetic message of Amos, is promised divine judgment. Because of His covenant, however, God will not abandon Israel altogether but will bring future restoration to the righteous remnant (see 9:7–15).

## INTERPRETIVE CHALLENGES

In Amos 9:11, the Lord promises that He "will raise up the tabernacle of David, which has fallen down." At the Jerusalem Council, convened to discuss whether Gentiles should be allowed into the church without requiring circumcision, James quoted this passage (see Acts 15:15–16) to support Peter's report of how God had "visited the Gentiles to take out of them a people for His name" (Acts 15:14). Some have thus concluded the passage was fulfilled in Jesus, the greater Son of David, through whom the dynasty of David was reestablished. The Acts reference, however, is best seen as an illustration of Amos's words and not the fulfillment. The temporal allusions to a future time ("On that day," 9:11), when Israel will "possess the remnant of Edom, and all the Gentiles" (9:12), when the Lord "will plant them in their land, and no longer shall they be pulled up from the land I have given them" (9:15), all make it clear that the prophet is speaking of Messiah's return at the Second Advent to sit upon the throne of David (see Isaiah 9:7), not the establishment of the church by the apostles.

# THE BOOK OF HOSEA

The title is derived from the main character and author of the book. The meaning of his name, "salvation," is the same as that of Joshua (see Numbers 13:8, 16) and Jesus (see Matthew 1:21). Hosea is the first of the twelve Minor Prophets. Once again, "minor" refers to the brevity of the prophecies, as compared to the length of the works of Isaiah, Jeremiah, and Ezekiel.

## AUTHOR AND DATE

The book of Hosea is the sole source of information about the author. Little is known about him, and even less is known about his father, Beeri (see Hosea 1:1).

Hosea was probably a native of the northern kingdom of Israel, since he shows familiarity with the history, circumstances, and topography of the north (see 4:15; 5:1, 13; 6:8–9; 10:5; 12:11–12; 14:6). This would make him and Jonah the only writing prophets from the northern kingdom. Although Hosea addressed both Israel (the northern kingdom) and Judah (the southern kingdom), he identified the king of Israel as "our king" (7:5). Hosea had a lengthy period of ministry, prophesying c. 755–710 BC, during the reigns of Uzziah (790–739 BC), Jotham (750–731 BC), Ahaz (735–715 BC), and Hezekiah (715–686 BC) in Judah, and Jeroboam II (793–753 BC) in Israel (see 1:1). His long career spanned the last six kings of Israel from Zechariah (753–752 BC) to Hoshea (732–722 BC). The overthrow of Zechariah (the last of the dynasty of Jehu) in 752 BC is depicted as yet future (see 1:4). Thus, he followed Amos's preaching in the north and was a contemporary of Isaiah and Micah as well, both of whom prophesied in Judah. Second Kings 14–20 and 2 Chronicles 26–32 record the historical period of Hosea's ministry.

## BACKGROUND AND SETTING

Hosea began his ministry to Israel (also called Ephraim, after its largest tribe) during the final days of Jeroboam II, under whose guidance Israel was enjoying both political peace and material prosperity as well as moral corruption and spiritual bankruptcy. However, upon Jeroboam II's death (753 BC), anarchy prevailed and Israel declined rapidly. Until her overthrow by Assyria thirty years later, four of Israel's six kings were assassinated by their successors. Prophesying during the days surrounding the fall of Samaria, Hosea focused on Israel's moral waywardness (see the book of Amos) and her breach of the covenantal relationship with the Lord, announcing that judgment was imminent. Circumstances were not much better in the southern kingdom. Usurping the priestly function, Uzziah had been struck with leprosy (see 2 Chronicles 26:16–21), and Jotham condoned idolatrous practices, opening the way for Ahaz to encourage Baal worship (see 2 Chronicles 27:1–28:4). Hezekiah's revival served only to slow Judah's acceleration toward a fate similar to that of her northern sister. Weak kings on both sides of the border repeatedly sought out alliances with their heathen neighbors (see Hosea 7:11; 2 Kings 15:19; 16:7) rather than seeking the Lord's help.

## HISTORICAL AND THEOLOGICAL THEMES

The theme of Hosea is God's loyal love for His covenant people, Israel, in spite of their idolatry. Thus, Hosea has been called the Saint John (the apostle of love) of the Old Testament. The Lord's true love for His people is unending and will tolerate no rival. Hosea's message contains much condemnation, both national and individual, but at the same time, he poignantly portrays the love of God toward His people with passionate emotion. Hosea was instructed by God to marry a certain woman and experience with her a domestic life that was a dramatization of the sin and unfaithfulness of Israel. The marital life of Hosea and his wife, Gomer, provide the rich metaphor that clarifies the themes of the book: sin, judgment, and forgiving love.

## INTERPRETIVE CHALLENGES

That the faithless wife, Gomer, is symbolic of faithless Israel is without doubt; but questions remain. First, some suggest the marital scenes in Hosea 1–3 should be taken only as allegory. However, there is nothing in the narrative, presented in simple prose, which would even question its literal occurrence. Much of its impact would be lost if not literal. When non-literal elements within the book are introduced, they are prefaced with "saw" (5:13; 9:10, 13), the normal Hebraic means of introducing non-literal scenes. Furthermore, there is no account of a prophet ever making himself the subject of an allegory or parable.

Second, some question the moral implications of God's command for Hosea to marry a prostitute. It appears best to see Gomer as chaste at the time of marriage to Hosea, only later having become an immoral woman. The words "take yourself a wife of harlotry" (1:2) are to be understood proleptically; that is, looking to the future. An immoral woman could not serve as a picture of Israel coming out of Egypt (see Hosea 2:15; 9:10), who then later wandered away from God (see 11:1). Chapter 3 describes Hosea taking back his wife, who had been rejected because of adultery, a rejection that was unjustifiable if Hosea had married a prostitute with full knowledge of her character.

A third question arises concerning the relationship between chapter 1 and chapter 3 and whether the woman of chapter 3 is Gomer or another woman. There are a number of factors which suggest that the woman of chapter 3 is Gomer. In Hosea 1:2, God's command is to "go, take"; in Hosea 3:1, however, His command is to "go again, love," suggesting that Hosea's love was to be renewed to the same woman. Furthermore, within the analogy of chapter 1, Gomer represents Israel. As God renews His love toward faithless Israel, so Hosea is to renew his love toward faithless Gomer. For chapter 3 to denote a different woman would confuse the analogy.

# Running from God's Will

## *Jonah 1:1–2:10*

## Drawing Near

What are some things you know with certainty that God wants you to accomplish right now?

_____

_____

_____

_____

_____

_____

_____

_____

_____

_____

_____

## The Context

As noted in the Introduction, the book of Jonah is part of the division in the Bible known as the "Minor Prophets." Once again, this designation is not meant to indicate that the messages of these prophets or their exploits are any less important than those of the "Major Prophets." Rather, the designation—which evidently goes back to Augustine (354–430 AD)—indicates the books are shorter than the relatively longer books of Isaiah, Ezekiel, Daniel, and Ezekiel.

The first thing to understand about Jonah is his status as a prophet. Jonah was among a select group of Israelites who had been set apart by God to live and speak as His representatives. While many of these prophets ministered to the people of Israel, the Lord sent Jonah to proclaim a message of divine judgment to the foreign nation. Jonah's call was in many ways similar to that of Jeremiah, who was told by God: "Behold, I have put My words in your mouth. See, I have this day set you over the nations and over the kingdoms, to root out and to pull down, to destroy and to throw down, to build and to plant" (Jeremiah 1:9–10).

Yet as we will see in the first two chapters of Jonah, these prophets of God were still human. They dealt with the corruption of sin, as we all do, and they retained the ability to reject God's will—even when they clearly understood the mandate they had received. In Jonah's case, this led him first to the port city of Joppa, where in disobedience he boarded a ship bound in the opposite direction, then into a storm, and finally into the belly of a "great fish" (Jonah 1:17), which God had prepared to remind his prophet of who was in charge.

## KEYS TO THE TEXT

Read Jonah 1:1–2:10, noting the key words and phrases indicated below.

> *THE COMMISSION OF JONAH: While other prophets prophesied against Gentile nations (such as Isaiah and Nahum), this is the only case of a prophet actually being sent to a foreign nation to deliver God's message against them.*

1:1. JONAH THE SON OF AMITTAI: Jonah's name is Hebrew for "dove," while that of his father means "truthful" or "loyal."

2. ARISE, GO TO NINEVEH: Jonah's ministry was for the salvation of that city, for the shame and jealousy of Israel, as well as a rebuke to the reluctance of the Jews to bring Gentiles to the true God. Nineveh, which dates back to Nimrod (see Genesis 10:11), was located on the banks of the Tigris River about five hundred miles northeast of Israel. It was always one of Assyria's royal cities and for many years served as the capital. The name Nineveh is thought to derive from "ninus" (i.e., Nimrod) and means the residence of Nimrod or "nunu" (Akkadian for "fish"). The people worshiped the fish goddess Nanshe (the daughter of Ea, the goddess of fresh water) and Dagon the fish god, who was represented as half man and half fish.

## THE GEOGRAPHY OF JONAH

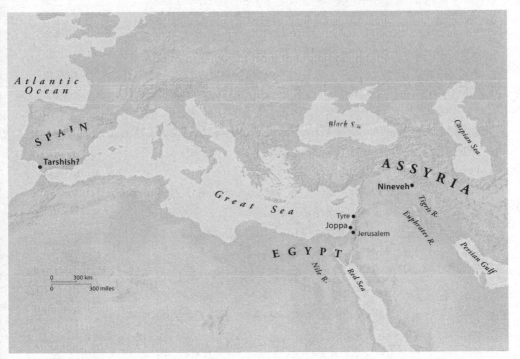

THAT GREAT CITY: Nineveh was great, both in terms of size (see Jonah 3:3) and in power, exerting significant influence over the Middle East until her destruction by Nebuchadnezzar in 612 BC. It was possibly the largest city in the world at this time. According to historians, magnificent walls almost eight miles long enveloped the inner city, with the rest of the city/district occupying an area with a circumference of some sixty miles. Its population could have approached 600,000 (see 4:11).

THEIR WICKEDNESS HAS COME UP BEFORE ME: Nineveh was the center of idolatrous worship of Assur and Ishtar. A century later, Nahum pronounced doom upon Assyria for her evil ways and cruelty (see Nahum 3), which was carried out by Nebuchadnezzar in 612 BC.

3. BUT JONAH AROSE TO FLEE TO TARSHISH: This is the only recorded instance of a prophet refusing God's commission (see Jeremiah 20:7–9). The location of Tarshish, famous for its wealth (see Psalm 72:10; Jeremiah 10:9; Ezekiel 27:12, 25), is not known for certain. The Greek historian Herodotus identified it with Tartessus, a merchant city in southern Spain, about 2,500 miles west of

Joppa. The prophet went as far west in the opposite direction as possible, showing his reluctance to bring salvation blessing to Gentiles.

FROM THE PRESENCE OF THE LORD: While no one can escape from the Lord's omnipresence (see Psalm 139:7–12; Amos 9:2–4), it is thought that the prophet was attempting to flee His manifest presence in the temple at Jerusalem (see Genesis 4:16; Jonah 2:4).

JOPPA: The city Joppa (today Jaffa), located on the Mediterranean coast near the border of Judah and Samaria, was also the location of Peter's vision in preparation for his visit to Cornelius, a Gentile (see Acts 10).

> THE PURSUIT OF JONAH: *The storm that Jonah encountered as a result of his disobedience was not an ordinary squall but an extreme one sent (literally "hurled") from God. Sailors, accustomed to storms, were afraid of this one.*

4. THE MARINERS WERE AFRAID: The sailors' fear served God's purpose (see Psalm 104:4). This is not unlike the apostle Paul's experience en route to Rome (see Acts 27:1–44).

5–6. HIS GOD . . . YOUR GOD: These sailors were hopelessly committed to a polytheistic belief system (in contrast to Jonah's monotheism), not unlike the Athenians in Paul's day, who believed in supernatural powers that intervened the course of natural laws (see Acts 17:23–24).

7. CAST LOTS: The last resort is to ascertain whose guilt has caused such divine anger. God could reveal His will by controlling the lots, which He did. This method of discernment by casting lots, the exact procedure of which is not known, was not forbidden in Israel (see Proverbs 16:33; Joshua 7:14ff.; 15:1; 1 Samuel 14:36–45; Acts 1:26).

8. PLEASE TELL US: What Jonah did not tell them was that he might have already known that Assyria would one day be victorious over Israel. Undoubtedly, Jonah's fierce natural pride clouded his prophet's commitment to God's divine appointment to evangelize Nineveh.

9. I AM A HEBREW: Jonah identified himself by the name that Israelites used among Gentiles (see 1 Samuel 4:6, 9; 14:11).

THE GOD OF HEAVEN: This title, in use from earliest times (see Genesis 24:3, 7), may have been specifically chosen by Jonah to express the sovereignty of the Lord in contrast to Baal, who was a sky god (see 1 Kings 18:24). Spoken to sailors who were most likely from Phoenicia, the center of Baal worship, the title bears significant weight, especially when coupled with the phrase "who made the sea and the dry land." This was the appropriate identification when introducing the true and living God to pagans who didn't have Scripture but whose reason led them to recognize the fact that there had to be a Creator (see Romans 1:18–23). To begin with creation, as in Acts 14:14–17 and 17:23b–29, was the proper starting point. To evangelize Jews, one can begin with the Old Testament Scripture.

11–12. THROW ME INTO THE SEA: Unwilling to go to Nineveh and feeling guilty, Jonah was willing to sacrifice himself in an effort to save the lives of others. Apparently, he would rather have died than go to Nineveh.

13–14. NEVERTHELESS THE MEN ROWED HARD: Heathen sailors had more concern for one man than Jonah had for tens of thousands in Nineveh. The storm, Jonah's words, and the lots all indicated to the sailors that the Lord was involved; thus, they offered sacrifices to Him and made vows, indicating Jonah had told them more about God than is recorded here.

15. THE SEA CEASED: The effect was similar to Christ's quieting the storm on the Sea of Galilee (see Matthew 8:23–27).

16. FEARED . . . EXCEEDINGLY: In Mark 4:41, the disciples also "feared exceedingly" when they witnessed Christ calming the sea. This was not fear of being harmed by the storm but a reverence for the supernatural power that Jesus had just displayed. The only thing more terrifying than having a storm outside the boat was having God in the boat!

17. A GREAT FISH: The species of fish is uncertain; the Hebrew word for whale is not here employed. God sovereignly prepared (literally "appointed") a great fish to rescue Jonah. Apparently Jonah sank into the depth of the sea before the fish swallowed him (see 2:3, 5–6).

THREE DAYS AND THREE NIGHTS: Jesus would later say to a group of scribes and Pharisees, "An evil and adulterous generation seeks after a sign, and no sign will be given to it except the sign of the prophet Jonah. For as Jonah was three days and three nights in the belly of the great fish, so will the Son of Man be three days and three nights in the heart of the earth" (Matthew 12:39–40). "Three days and three nights" was an emphatic way of saying "three days," and by Jewish reckoning, an apt way of expressing a period of time that included parts of three days. Thus, if Christ was crucified on a Friday, and His resurrection occurred on the first day of the week, by Hebrew reckoning this would qualify as three days and three nights.

> THE DELIVERANCE: *Jonah's prayer acknowledged God's sovereignty and his submission to it. His prayer under duress stands in contrast to prayers of obedient men in Scripture, such as Daniel and Nehemiah.*

2:2. OUT OF THE BELLY OF SHEOL: The phrase does not necessarily indicate that Jonah actually died. Sheol frequently has a hyperbolic meaning in contexts where it denotes a catastrophic condition near death (see Psalm 30:3). Later, Jonah expressed praise for his deliverance "from the pit," speaking of his escape from otherwise certain death.

3. YOU CAST ME INTO THE DEEP: In describing his watery experience, Jonah acknowledged that his circumstances were a judgment from the Lord.

4. I HAVE BEEN CAST OUT OF YOUR SIGHT: In Jonah 1:3, the prophet ran from God's presence; here, he realized that the Lord had temporarily expelled him.

YOUR HOLY TEMPLE: Jonah expressed confidence that he would one day see and be in the sight of God, possibly in Jerusalem but more likely in heaven (see verse 7).

5. EVEN TO MY SOUL: This describes Jonah's total person—both physically and spiritually.

9. I HAVE VOWED: Jonah found himself in the same position as the mariners: offering sacrifices and making vows (see 1:16). In light of Jonah 3:1–4, his vow could well have been to carry out God's ministry will for him by preaching in Nineveh (see Psalms 50:14; 66:13–14).

SALVATION IS OF THE LORD: See Psalm 3:8 and Isaiah 45:17. The God of Israel is the only Savior (see Isaiah 43:11; Hosea 13:4; Jude 1:25).

10. THE LORD SPOKE: Just as God spoke the world into existence (see Genesis 1:3, 6, 9, 11, 14, 20, 24) and calls the stars by name (see Isaiah 40:26; Psalm 147:4), so He speaks to His creation in the animal world (see Numbers 22:28–30). Most likely, Jonah was vomited upon the shore of Palestine, possibly near Joppa.

## UNLEASHING THE TEXT

1)  In your own words, what did God command Jonah to do in 1:1–2?

_____

_____

_____

_____

_____

2) What do you learn about Jonah's character and motivations in chapters 1 and 2?

_____

_____

_____

_____

_____

_____

3) What do you learn about God's character and motivations from those chapters?

_____

_____

_____

_____

_____

_____

4) How would you summarize the message of Jonah's psalm in chapter 2?

_____

_____

_____

_____

_____

## EXPLORING THE MEANING

***God has a specific plan for the world.*** The first truth we glean from Jonah's story is one that is repeated continually and consistently throughout Scripture; namely, that God has precise plans and goals that He desires to be accomplished in this world. God first announced these plans through the act of creation—through His conception and construction of the physical world, including humanity. God further solidified the reality of His will through the process of revelation. He did not allow circumstances to unfold by chance but intervened to reveal Himself to people at specific times—Adam, Abraham, Moses, David, and so on. God's revelation to His people has always been personal and instructional. He reveals not only who He is but also what He wants His people to do. Finally, note that

God's revealed will in the book of Jonah goes beyond the prophet as an individual. Yes, it was God's plan for Jonah to "Arise, go to Nineveh, that great city, and cry out against it" (Jonah 1:2). But that was not the extent of God's plan. He also desired for the people of Nineveh to hear the word of the Lord—and to repent.

*God has sovereign power to bring about His will.* God designed us with the ability to choose and make decisions, so we can understand the reality of God's will in this world in a small way. Like our Creator, we have the ability to develop preferences, plans, desires, and designs (see Proverbs 16:9). But this is where the similarities end, for the Bible also reveals that God's thoughts and His ways are higher than our own (see Isaiah 55:8–9). Furthermore, as we see in Jonah 1, God has the perfect ability to bring about His will through His sovereign power. God not only makes plans, but He also makes them happen. He possesses the resources to accomplish whatever He desires—which can include sovereignly arranging "a great wind," controlling the outcome of sailors casting lots, and miraculously providing a "great fish" to swallow His servant. Notice that God's sovereignty is not limited by the will of human beings. In fact, God predestined to accomplish His purposes through the actions of men. Jonah desired to disobey God; that was his will, and he attempted to act on it. Yet God worked through the circumstances in Jonah's life so as to accomplish His sovereign plan.

*Compassion is a worthy virtue for God's people.* There is a striking comparison between Jonah and the sailors that is worth a deeper exploration. Specifically, the sailors demonstrated a level of compassion that put Jonah—the declared "Hebrew" and prophet of God—to shame. Jonah's lack of compassion is first seen in his decision to disobey God. His hatred toward the Assyrian people was so intense that he knowingly risked God's discipline by fleeing in the opposite direction from Nineveh and making for Tarshish. Even while he was in the middle of the tempest, there is no indication that Jonah's hatred for the Ninevites relented—he was willing to die in the sea rather than preach the word of the Lord to that city. By comparison, the sailors on board Jonah's hired vessel had no knowledge of the true God and His character, yet they imitated the Almighty. God expressed His compassion for the people of Nineveh (and by extension, Assyria) by sending a prophet to call them to repentance. Similarly, the sailors extended great compassion toward Jonah by doing everything possible to spare his life in a moment of extreme danger. May we also imitate our God who is "full of compassion, and gracious" (Psalm 86:15).

## REFLECTING ON THE TEXT

5) What verses come to mind that inform your understanding of God's will? Do you submit to what He has revealed?

_____

_____

_____

_____

_____

6) When have you experienced a dissonance between God's will and your own? Describe the consequences you've endured when you defy His will.

_____

_____

_____

_____

_____

7) What is the relationship between our will and God's sovereignty? Does God ordain the end as well as the means to that end?

_____

_____

_____

_____

_____

8) What are some ways that God has demonstrated compassion toward you?

_____

_____

_____

_____

_____

## PERSONAL RESPONSE

9)   In what ways are you attempting to flee from God's will? Why?

_____

_____

_____

_____

_____

_____

_____


10) What are some of the ways that God has shown you compassion when you did
    not deserve it?

_____

_____

_____

_____

_____

_____

_____

# 2

# FULFILLING GOD'S WILL
*Jonah 3:1–4:11*

## DRAWING NEAR

Consider God's patience toward you. How does this impact your worship of Him?

_____

_____

_____

_____

_____

_____

_____

_____

_____

_____

## THE CONTEXT

Jonah had been instructed by God to travel to Nineveh, the capital city of Assyria, and confront the wickedness of its people. The city of Nineveh was approximately 550 miles northeast of Jonah's likely location in Israel, which would have required a long journey over land. But instead of obeying God's call, Jonah fled to Joppa and booked passage on a ship bound for Tarshish—a city likely in the exact opposite direction from Nineveh. In other words, Jonah attempted to flee as far away as he possibly could from God's mission for his life.

In the end, however, God's will prevailed. "The LORD sent out a great wind on the sea, and there was a mighty tempest on the sea, so that the ship was about to be broken up" (Jonah 1:4). The sailors cast lots and found that Jonah was the cause of the storm, eventually prompting them (at the prophet's insistence) to throw him overboard. The Lord sent a great fish to swallow Jonah . . . but the prophet did not die. Instead, he remained in the belly of the fish three days and three nights, where he cried out to God for salvation.

God answered Jonah's prayer by causing the fish to vomit him on dry land, most likely on the shore of Palestine and possibly near the city of Joppa where he had started. The third chapter in Jonah describes God's renewal of His commission to His prophet—one that this time was accepted and obeyed. Jonah went to Nineveh and proclaimed the Word of the Lord to great effect. However, the final chapter makes it clear that Jonah himself had a long way to go in terms of conforming his heart and values to those of his heavenly Father.

## KEYS TO THE TEXT

Read Jonah 3:1–4:11, noting the key words and phrases indicated below.

> *THE PROPHET OBEYS: God gives Jonah a second chance and again commissions him to go to Nineveh and preach a message of repentance.*

3.1. THE SECOND TIME: As noted previously, Jonah is the only prophet actually sent by God to preach repentance in a foreign land. Jonah is also the only prophet recorded in Scripture who refused God's commission, so God made this unique calling to him twice. The prophet was to travel more than 500 miles from where he landed on the shore near Joppa to Nineveh.

3. AN EXCEEDINGLY GREAT CITY: Literally "a great city to God." The text emphasizes not only the city's great size (see Jonah 1:2) but also its importance (see 4:11).

A THREE-DAY JOURNEY: A metropolitan city the size of Nineveh, with a circumference of about sixty miles, would require three days just to get around it. These dimensions are confirmed by historians. Stopping to preach would only add to the time requirement.

4. YET FORTY DAYS: The time frame may harken back to Moses's supplication for forty days and nights at Sinai (see Deuteronomy 9:18, 25). Jonah's message, while short, accomplishes God's intended purpose.

*THE CITY REPENTS: Jonah's experience with the fish, in light of the Ninevites' pagan beliefs, would have gained him an instant hearing. This wholesale repentance was a miraculous work of God.*

5. THE PEOPLE . . . BELIEVED GOD: Jesus would later use the Ninevites' repentance at the lesser prophet Jonah to condemn the Pharisees' rejection of Jesus, a greater one than Jonah (see Matthew 12:41; Luke 11:32). Pagan sailors and a pagan city responded to the reluctant prophet, showing the power of God in spite of His servant's weakness.

6. THE KING OF NINEVEH: The king of Nineveh—thought by some to be Adad-nirari III (c. 810–783 BC), but much more likely Assurdan III (c. 772–755 BC)— exchanged his royal robes for sackcloth and ashes (compare Job 42:6 and Isaiah 58:5). Reports of Jonah's miraculous fish experience may have preceded him to Nineveh, accounting for the swift and widespread receptivity of his message (see Jonah 1:2). It is generally believed that acid from the fish's stomach would have bleached Jonah's face, thus validating the experience.

7–9. MAN NOR BEAST: It was a Persian custom to use animals in mourning ceremonies.

10. GOD SAW . . . GOD RELENTED: The Ninevites truly repented, which is what Jonah did not want to happen (see Jonah 4:2). Thus, the Assyrian nation could be used one generation later as the rod of God's anger (see Isaiah 10:5) as foretold by Isaiah, Hosea, and Amos.

*JONAH QUESTIONS GOD'S WILL: Jonah, because of his rejection of Gentiles and distaste for their participation in salvation, was displeased at God's demonstration of mercy toward the Ninevites— thereby displaying the actual reason for his original flight to Tarshish—and questioned God's plans.*

4:1. IT DISPLEASED JONAH EXCEEDINGLY: From the very beginning, Jonah had clearly understood the gracious character of God (see 1 Timothy 2:4; 2 Peter 3:9). He had received pardon but didn't want Nineveh to know God's mercy (see a similar attitude in Luke 15:25ff.). Jonah was much like the Pharisees of Jesus' day (see Matthew 12:41; Luke 11:34).

2. GRACIOUS . . . LOVINGKINDNESS: These are well-documented attributes of God (see Exodus 34:6; Numbers 14:18; Psalms 86:15; 103:8; 145:8–9). The

prophet Joel declared, "He is gracious and merciful, slow to anger, and of great kindness; and He relents from doing harm" (Joel 2:13).

3. BETTER . . . TO DIE: Perhaps Jonah was expressing the reality of breaking his vow (see Jonah 2:9) to God a second time (see Numbers 30:2; Ecclesiastes 5:1–6). Jonah joined the ranks of Job (see Job 6:8–9), Moses (see Numbers 11:10–15), and Elijah (see 1 Kings 19:4) in wanting to die. (See also Jonah 4:8.)

4. RIGHT . . . ANGRY: See verse 1. Jonah's anger was kindled because his will did not prevail; rather, God's will did (see Matthew 26:39, 42). Jonah apparently gave no answer.

6. A PLANT: The identity of this plant is uncertain, but it possibly could be the fast-growing castor oil plant, which in hot climates grows rapidly to give shade with its large leaves.

8. VEHEMENT EAST WIND: A hot, scorching wind, normally called "sirocco," blowing off the Arabian desert. The shelter Jonah made for himself (see verse 5) would not exclude this "agent" of God's sovereignty.

9. ANGRY, EVEN TO DEATH: Jonah's anger had reached the point of being irrational, as God describes in verse 10. James 1:19–20 expresses the antidote for Jonah's emotional poison.

10–11. SHOULD I NOT PITY NINEVEH: God's love for the people of Nineveh, whom He had created, is far different from Jonah's indifference to their damnation and greater than Jonah's warped concern for a wild plant's shade for which he had done nothing worthy to deserve it.

ONE HUNDRED AND TWENTY THOUSAND: God was ready to spare Sodom for ten righteous people; how much more a city that includes 120,000 small children, identified as those who cannot discern the right hand from the left (see Genesis 18:22–23). With that many three- or four-year-old children, it is reasonable to expect a total population in excess of 600,000. Jonah's preaching certainly equaled, if not eclipsed, Peter's ministry at Pentecost (see Acts 2:14–39).

## UNLEASHING THE TEXT

1)   What did God command Jonah to do in 3:1–2?

_____

_____

_____

_____

_____

2) What is the evidence of revival and spiritual fruit in 3:5–10?

_____

_____

_____

_____

_____

_____

3) What are some words you would use to describe Jonah's actions and attitudes in chapter 4?

_____

_____

_____

_____

_____

_____

4) What are the similarities between Jonah's mission and our mission as modern-day disciples of Christ?

_____

_____

_____

_____

_____

_____

## EXPLORING THE MEANING

***Our heavenly Father is a gracious and patient God.*** As you read through Jonah, it's difficult to miss the similarities between the two commissions that God delivered to His prophet: "Now the word of the LORD came to Jonah the son of Amittai, saying, 'Arise, go to Nineveh, that great city, and cry out against it; for their wickedness has come up before Me' " (1:1–2); "Now the word of the LORD came to Jonah the second time, saying, 'Arise, go to Nineveh, that great city, and preach to it the message that I tell you' " (3:1–2). Jonah's second chance was a tangible reflection of God's grace and patience. The prophet had already failed in following God's first command by attempting to run away from the Lord's will—something Jonah should have known to be impossible. Even so, God showed mercy to His prophet. God also showed mercy to the people of Nineveh, who were renowned for their wickedness. Jonah's declaration—"Yet forty days, and Nineveh shall be overthrown!" (3:4)—was not a bluff. The Assyrians were deserving of God's wrath, yet, due to His grace, God granted them salvation, which they did not deserve.

*Repentance requires action.* In chapter 3, we witness the effects of Jonah's prophetic message: "So the people of Nineveh believed God" (verse 5). It is quite likely that the Assyrians had heard about Jonah's miraculous survival in the belly of the great fish prior to his arrival, which may explain why they were so receptive to his message. As a result, the Bible states that they "believed." Importantly, however, their belief was not merely a mental assent. They did not agree with Jonah and then continue with their normal sinful lives. Instead, their belief was accompanied by actions that expressed their repentance. From the least to the greatest, the Ninevites fasted. They wore sackcloth to depict their sorrow and penitence. They cried out to God. Most critically, "Every one turn[ed] from his evil way and from the violence that is in his hands" (verse 8). In other words, the Ninevites' actions after hearing Jonah's message showed their newfound faith was authentic. This reality reflects God's message through the apostle James, who wrote, "Thus also faith by itself, if it does not have works, is dead" (James 2:17).

*Our commission is likewise to share the gospel with those who need it.* The Assyrians were locked in a cultural pattern of paganism and violence. They did not know God and had no hope of reaching Him without His direct intervention. For that reason, the Lord gave a special commission to Jonah and instructed him to share the truth with this people group who were mired in their own wickedness. The same is true for every follower of Jesus today. Prior to Jesus' ascension, He gave this command to all who chose to follow Him: "Go therefore and make disciples of all nations, baptizing them in the name of the Father and of the Son and of the Holy Spirit, teaching them to observe all things that I have commanded you; and lo, I am with you always, even to the end of the age" (Matthew 28:19–20). Like Jonah, we are surrounded by people suffering the consequences of their own unrighteousness and rebellion against God. Such people are lost without God's grace and have no hope for salvation. Also like Jonah, our command is to go and proclaim God's Word to these people who need to hear it.

## REFLECTING ON THE TEXT

5)   What do you learn about God's character from Jonah's message to the Ninevites?

_____

_____

_____

_____

_____

6)   What does it mean to "believe" the message of the gospel?

_____

_____

_____

_____

_____

7)   What are some actions or lifestyle changes that accompany salvation?

_____

_____

_____

_____

_____

8)   Look again at Jesus' Great Commission in Matthew 28:18–20. What is your responsibility as a Christian concerning the lost?

_____

_____

_____

_____

_____

## PERSONAL RESPONSE

9) Are you currently in danger of displaying an attitude of insubordination and callousness, similar to Jonah's, toward God and the lost?

_____

_____

_____

_____

_____

_____

_____

_____

10) Where do you have an opportunity this week to share the gospel with someone who needs to hear it?

_____

_____

_____

_____

_____

_____

_____

# 3

# JUDGMENTS AGAINST THE NATIONS

*Amos 1:1–2:16*

## DRAWING NEAR

When have you recently dealt with the consequences of a poor choice or a foolish decision?

_____

_____

_____

_____

_____

_____

_____

_____

_____

_____

## THE CONTEXT

In the previous session, we saw that Jonah ministered during the reign of Jeroboam II, "the son of Joash" (2 Kings 14:23), who ruled in Israel c. 793–753 BC. This king's greatest accomplishment was the restoration of Israel's boundaries to approximately their extent in Solomon's time, excluding territory belonging to Judah. The territorial expansion was in accordance with the will of the Lord, "which He had spoken through His servant Jonah the son of Amittai" (verse 25).

The opening chapter of Amos reveals he also prophesized "in the days of Jeroboam the son of Joash" (Amos 1:1), making him a contemporary of Jonah. As we discussed, the nation was enjoying a time of peace and prosperity during Jeroboam II's lengthy forty-one-year reign, but spiritually, it was a time of great poverty for the nation. This compelled the Lord, in His mercy, to send prophets to warn the people of the judgment that would fall if they did not turn from their idolatrous ways. Thus, we find not only Jonah and Amos ministering during this time but also the prophets Hosea (see Hosea 1:1) and Isaiah (see Isaiah 1:1).

Amos, a Judean sheepbreeder raised in a village ten miles south of Jerusalem, was called by God to prophesy away from his homeland in this northern kingdom of Israel. As with most prophets, he confronted regions and nations with the reality of their sin and rebellion against the Lord. But the purpose of Amos's prophetic proclamations were more than punitive, for God sent Amos as a vehicle of His grace. His message of judgment was intended to highlight the consequences of the people's wickedness and offer them the opportunity to repent.

## KEYS TO THE TEXT

Read Amos 1:1–2:16, noting the key words and phrases indicated below.

> *JUDGMENTS AGAINST ISRAEL'S ENEMIES: Amos begins his prophecy with Israel's enemies, which gains him an initial hearing. But later, when he turns to God's judgment on Israel, the leaders will try to silence him (see Amos 7:10–17).*

1:1. AMOS . . . AMONG THE SHEEPBREEDERS: As stated in the Introduction, Amos was the only prophet to announce his occupation before declaring his divine commission.

THE EARTHQUAKE: This earthquake, mentioned by Zechariah (see 14:5) and Josephus (see *Antiquities*, IX.10.4), connects it with Uzziah's sin of usurping the role of a priest (see 2 Chronicles 26:16–23). An earthquake of severe magnitude occurred in the region c. 750 BC, although it cannot be precisely dated.

2. ROARS: In Joel 3:16, the Lord roars against the nations; here, His wrath was directed primarily toward Israel (see Jeremiah 25:30). Amos, a shepherd, courageously warned the flock of God's pasture that they were in imminent danger from a roaring lion, who turned out to be the ultimate Shepherd of the flock (see Amos 3:8).

MOURN . . . WITHERS: This is a message of destructive judgment.

CARMEL: Known for its bountiful trees and lush gardens, Carmel means "fertility" or "garden land" and refers to the mountain range that runs east to west in northern Israel, jutting out into the Mediterranean Sea (see 9:3).

3. FOR THREE TRANSGRESSIONS . . . FOR FOUR: This rhetorical device is repeated as an introduction in each of the eight messages (see 1:3–2:16), differing from a similar pattern used elsewhere (see Job 5:19; Psalm 62:11; Proverbs 30:15). These are specific mathematical enumerations (see Proverbs 30:18, 21, 29), emphasizing that each nation was being visited for an incalculable number of infractions. With three, the cup of iniquity was full; with four it overflowed. This judgment was to fall on Syria, whose capital is Damascus.

THRESHED GILEAD: Large threshing sleds which, when dragged over grain, would both thresh the grain and cut the straw. Gilead, located in the northeastern Golan Heights region of Israel, was vulnerable to Syria's cruel attacks (see 2 Kings 13:7; 18:12).

4. BEN-HADAD: Apparently a throne name, meaning "son of (the god) Hadad." Ben-Hadad II was a son of the Syrian king Hazael (841–801 BC).

5. VALLEY OF AVEN: Meaning "valley of wickedness," it may refer to Baalbek, the center of sun worship, located north of Damascus.

BETH EDEN: "House of pleasure." It was located in eastern Syria across the Euphrates River.

KIR: Apparently the original home of the Syrians. It was a region to which they were later exiled (see 2 Kings 16:9). Its exact location is unknown.

6. GAZA: Philistia's most prominent merchant city, ideally situated between Egypt and Israel, here used to refer to the Philistine nation.

TOOK CAPTIVE THE WHOLE CAPTIVITY: The Philistines deported an entire population (see Jeremiah 13:19), possibly during the reign of Jehoram (see 2 Chronicles 21:16, 17; Joel 3:3), c. 853–841 BC.

EDOM: The Edomites trace their origin to Esau, firstborn son of Isaac and Rebekah (see Genesis 25:22–26). Israel and Edom were perpetual enemies. When Israel came out from Egypt, Edom denied them passage through their land (see Numbers 20:14–21). They opposed Saul (c. 1043–1011 BC) and were subdued under David (c. 1011–971 BC) and Solomon (c. 971–931 BC). They fought against Jehoshaphat (c. 873–848 BC) and successfully rebelled against Jehoram (c. 853–841 BC). They would again be conquered by Judah under Amaziah (c. 796–767 BC) but would regain their freedom during the reign of Ahaz (c. 735–715 BC).

**7–8. GAZA . . . ASHDOD . . . ASHKELON . . . EKRON:** Four of the five major cities of Philistia. The fifth city, Gath, was not mentioned by Amos because it had been destroyed earlier by Uzziah (see 2 Chronicles 26:6).

**9. COVENANT OF BROTHERHOOD:** A long-standing brotherly relationship existed between Phoenicia and Israel, beginning with King Hiram's assistance to David in building his house (see 2 Samuel 5:11) and Solomon in building the temple (see 1 Kings 5:1–12; 9:11–14), and later solidified through the marriage of Jezebel to Ahab (see 1 Kings 16:31). No king of Israel ever made war against Phoenicia, especially the two major cities, Tyre and Sidon.

**10. TYRE:** Alexander the Great would later conquer this stronghold c. 330 BC (see Ezekiel 26:1–18).

**11. PURSUED . . . CAST OFF ALL PITY:** More than mere fighting, Edom pursued his brother (i.e., Israel), stifling any feelings of compassion. The prophet Obadiah provided a more complete explanation of Edom's judgment, stating that it would "be cut off forever" (Obadiah 1:10) and "no survivor shall remain of the house of Esau" (verse 18). Ironically, the Edomites would applaud the destruction of Jerusalem by the Babylonians in 586 BC (see Psalm 137:7) but would die trying to defend it during the Jewish-Roman wars in AD 70. After that time, just as God had decreed through Obadiah, they were never heard of again.

**12. TEMAN:** The grandson of Esau (see Genesis 36:11), after whom this town in northern Edom was named.

**BOZRAH.** A fortress city of northern Edom, about thirty-five miles north of Petra.

**13. PEOPLE OF AMMON:** Descendants of Ben-Ammi, the son of Lot and his younger daughter (see Genesis 19:34–38).

**RIPPED OPEN THE WOMEN WITH CHILD:** Such inhumane treatment in wartime was not an uncommon practice (see 2 Kings 8:12; 15:16; Hosea 13:16).

**GILEAD:** See note on verse 3.

**14. RABBAH:** Situated east of the Jordan River, this was the capital city.

**15. THEIR KING SHALL GO INTO CAPTIVITY:** The Assyrian king, Tiglath-Pileser III, carried out this destruction c. 734 BC.

**2:1. MOAB:** Descendants of Lot and his elder daughter (see Genesis 19:37).

**BURNED THE BONES:** This event, where vengeance didn't stop at death, is not recorded elsewhere in Scripture.

**2. KERIOTH:** An important Moabite city, either as a capital or as a center of worship.

3. JUDGE: Possibly denoting the king, who was often so designated (see 2 Kings 15:5; Daniel 9:12).

*JUDGMENT AGAINST JUDAH AND ISRAEL: With judgments against the surrounding pagan nations finished, the prophet addresses Judah, moving ever closer to his ultimate target of prophesying against Israel.*

4. DESPISED THE LAW OF THE LORD: The nations were judged because they had sinned against the law of God, which was written in their hearts and in their consciences (see Romans 2:14–15). Judah and Israel were judged because they had sinned against the Lord's revealed written law. (See also the warnings of Deuteronomy 28:15–68.)

5. FIRE UPON JUDAH: The Babylonian king Nebuchadnezzar fulfilled this judgment c. 605–586 BC (see 2 Kings 24–25).

6–7. TRANSGRESSIONS OF JUDAH: Greed summarizes Judah's transgressions. It was so all-consuming that for insignificant debts the people of Israel would sell another into slavery (see Matthew 18:23–35), and it was accompanied by uncontained sexual passion. Care for the poor is a prominent Old Testament theme (e.g., Proverbs 14:31; 17:5), and sexual purity is mandated repeatedly (see Leviticus 18). Violations of both are an affront to God's holy name.

GO IN TO THE SAME GIRL: In the context of oppressing the helpless, the reference was probably to a slave girl (see Exodus 21:7–11).

8. CLOTHES TAKEN IN PLEDGE: Outer garments used to secure a loan were to be returned before sunset (see Exodus 22:25–27; Deuteronomy 24:12–13) and a widow's garment was not to be taken under any circumstance (see Deuteronomy 24:17); but instead, the people of Judah were using them to engage in idolatrous acts.

THE WINE OF THE CONDEMNED: They used the wine bought with unjustly extracted fines from the poor to engage in forbidden worship, thus sinning twice against the Lord.

9. AMORITE: The pre-Conquest inhabitants of Canaan, whom God defeated for the Jews (see Joshua 10:12–15).

HEIGHT . . . STRONG: Their giant stature was said to make the Exodus spies look like grasshoppers (see Numbers 13:32–33). God will destroy them completely—both fruit and root (see Ezekiel 17:9; Malachi 4:1).

11. NAZIRITES: See Numbers 6:1–21.

**12. GAVE THE NAZIRITES WINE TO DRINK:** The Nazirite separated himself to the Lord by separating himself from (1) grape products (see Numbers 6:3–4), (2) the cutting of his hair (see 6:5), and (3) contact with a dead body (see 6:6–7). Like the high priest, the Nazirite was considered holy to the Lord (see 6:8; Exodus 28:36) all the days of his vow.

**13. WEIGHED DOWN:** The context of verses 14–16 determines the exact meaning of verse 13, which is elusive. These three verses essentially predict that Israel will be severely impeded from fleeing the impending divine judgment for their sins (see verses 6–12). There are two possible understandings of verse 13: (1) God will crush the Israelites under His divine judgment in much the same manner as a person would be severely injured if struck and crushed by a moving, fully loaded cart; or (2) God will providentially press down on Israel, unlike when they were free to sin, so they cannot flee or escape from the invading nation that will inflict God's judgment, most likely Assyria in 722 BC. The intended parallel idea would be that as God bogged down Israel (so she could not flee) because of her sin, so a cart would be immovable if overloaded with sheaves. The latter of these interpretations is preferable in this context, since the idea is rendering Israel vulnerable to attack not directly inflicting the judgment.

**14–16. SHALL PERISH:** Neither personal strength nor military armament was sufficient to prevent the Lord's hand of judgment by the Assyrians c. 722 BC (see 2 Kings 17).

## UNLEASHING THE TEXT

1) According to Amos 1, what had the nations done to arouse God's anger?

_____

_____

_____

_____

_____

2) What do you learn about God based on the judgments pronounced by Amos?

_____

_____

_____

_____

_____

3) According to Amos 2, what had the people of Israel and Judah done to arouse God's anger?

_____

_____

_____

_____

_____

_____

_____

4) Why is God's wrath a necessary expression of His justice?

_____

_____

_____

_____

_____

_____

## EXPLORING THE MEANING

**God will judge humanity.** One thing the writings of the prophets make clear is that God will judge humanity—and to do so in both senses of that word. First, God will preside as the Judge over humanity. He has delivered His standards and expectations, and He alone carries the authority to determine whether individuals and nations have rightly conformed to that standard. He sits in judgment over all people. Second, God will render judgment upon humanity in the sense of assigning and implementing consequences. When nations and individuals rebel against God, they can be assured of experiencing His judgment, both temporal on earth and everlasting in hell. God alone has the authority and ability to punish sinners with true justice. We see both aspects of God's judgment at work in Amos 1–2. Each of the eight judgments pronounced by the prophet in these chapters begins with the words, "Thus says the LORD." God was operating in the role of Judge by evaluating not only individual people but also entire nations. In addition, each of the eight judgments pronounced by Amos includes divinely appointed consequences: "I will cut off the inhabitant from Ashdod" (1:8). . . . "But I will kindle a fire in the wall of Rabbah, and it shall devour its palaces" (1:14). . . . "Therefore flight shall perish from the swift, the strong shall not strengthen his power, nor shall the mighty deliver himself" (2:14).

*God's judgments are always deserved.* Throughout history, cultures have told stories about false gods who were capricious in nature. These gods were petty, violent, and vengeful without cause and commonly carried out punishments that were undeserved. Even in Western culture today, there is a sense that God (or some version of a generic deity) delivers punishments in ways that are haphazard. But none of these attributes can be applied to the God of the Bible. Instead, He operates as a just Judge who carries out His judgments with fairness. We see this in Amos 1–2, where each of the judgments pronounced by the prophet makes it clear how a specific region or nation transgressed against God and earned His wrath. For instance, in pronouncing judgment against Ammon, God clearly reported its crime: "Because they ripped open the women with child in Gilead, that they might enlarge their territory" (1:13). Their brutality against the innocent brought consequences. In addition, each judgment in Amos 1–2 contains the rhetorical phrase, "for three transgressions . . . for four." This shows that God was not pronouncing judgment against isolated mistakes but for repeated transgressions.

*God's judgments also apply to His people.* As we consider God's justice and fairness as a Judge over humanity, it is important to note His willingness to extend that judgment over His own people. In the days of Abraham, the Lord made His love clear for His people by setting them apart for Himself. As God told the Israelites of Moses's day, "The LORD did not set His love on you nor choose you because you were more in number than any other people, for you were the least of all peoples; but because the LORD loves you, and because He would keep the oath which He swore to your fathers" (Deuteronomy 7:7–8). God established a unique connection with the descendants of Abraham through whom He brought forth the Messiah. Even so, God's affection for Israel did not mean that He ignored their transgressions, nor did it spur Him to neglect the consequences of His judgment that they had earned. While Amos 1:1–2:3 details judgments against nations and regions surrounding God's people, Amos 2:4–16 includes pronouncements against Israel and Judah. God rightly judged those He had set apart as His own—and He continues to do so in the church today, albeit as a disciplinary action of a loving Father. While followers of Jesus are not in danger of eternal consequences, we do still bring discipline upon ourselves when we choose to transgress God's standards.

## REFLECTING ON THE TEXT

5)  Why is it good news that God presides as the true Judge over humanity?

_____

_____

_____

_____

_____

_____

6)  What is the evidence of God's justice in Amos 1–2?

_____

_____

_____

_____

_____

7)  What is the evidence of God's fairness in those same chapters?

_____

_____

_____

_____

_____

8)  Look at the judgments against Israel and Judah in Amos 2:4–16. What can you learn about God's values by examining the transgressions listed in those verses?

_____

_____

_____

_____

_____

## PERSONAL RESPONSE

9) God's character has ample room for both justice and grace. How have those two attributes been displayed in your life?

_____

_____

_____

_____

_____

_____

_____

_____

10) What steps can you take to become more aware of those moments when you are in danger of violating God's standards?

_____

_____

_____

_____

_____

_____

_____

# 4

# CONDEMNATIONS AGAINST ISRAEL

## Amos 3:1 6:14

## DRAWING NEAR

When has someone recently offered you a word of critique or rebuke? How did you respond?

_____

_____

_____

_____

_____

_____

_____

_____

_____

_____

_____

## THE CONTEXT

As we consider the book of Amos, it's important to remember the prophet delivered these words in a specific place to a specific people. He verbally pronounced God's words of divine judgment to the leaders of Israel's northern kingdom in the city of Bethel (see Amos 7:10–13). This means that Amos didn't have the luxury of writing a scathing article and posting it anonymously for others to read— he personally witnessed the reactions to his words.

As noted previously, Amos began his proclamation by speaking judgments against Israel's enemies. In doing so, he was likely welcomed with a positive response. The leaders of Israel would have been only too pleased to hear about the impending destruction of their neighboring enemies—the Syrians, Philistines, Phoenicians, Edomites, Ammonites, and Moabites—all of whom had caused turmoil in their history. They likely would have even applauded God's judgment on Judah because of the hostility between the two nations.

But while Amos began the prophecy with pronouncements against distant lands from Israel (like Damascus and the Philistine territories), with each judgment from God, he progressively moved closer to the nation's borders. The judgment against Judah revealed that God would not play favorites, for although the nations shared a common religious heritage, the Lord would not allow its idolatry to continue. Now, as we move into chapters 3 to 6, we see Amos turn his attention fully to Israel and proclaim God's judgments against its people. Specifically, God condemns them for their irresponsibility, idolatry, and moral/ethical decay.

## KEYS TO THE TEXT

Read Amos 3:1–6:1, noting the key words and phrases indicated below.

> SIN OF IRRESPONSIBILITY: *The primary recipients of these messages delivered by the prophet Amos were the people of Israel, although the people of Judah were not excluded.*

3:2. YOU ONLY HAVE I KNOWN: This "knowing" refers to an intimate relationship, not just awareness (see Genesis 4:1, 17; Matthew 1:25; John 10:14–15). But God's sovereign choice of Israel did not exempt her from punishment for disobedience (see Deuteronomy 28:15–68).

3–8. CAN TWO WALK TOGETHER: The Lord posed a series of rhetorical questions to show that, as some things are certain in nature, surely nothing happens in Israel that is outside His sovereignty. Certain actions have predictable results. The Lord had spoken a word; therefore, the prophet was to speak and the people were to listen with trembling. Instead, they tried the impossible—that is, to silence the prophet (see Amos 2:12; 7:12–13)—and effectively silence God.

7. THE LORD GOD DOES NOTHING: Judgment is coming, but the Lord graciously warned the nation in advance through His prophets (e.g., Noah in Genesis 6; Abraham in Genesis 18).

8. LION HAS ROARED: As it is with the king of the wild, it is much more so with the King of creation (see Amos 1:3).

9. PROCLAIM IN THE PALACES: The heathen nations, such as the Philistines and Egyptians, were divinely summoned to witness God's judgment of Israel (see verse 13). If even they condemn Israel, how much more will a righteous God?

11. AN ADVERSARY: This would be the Assyrians, who captured and deported Israel in 722 BC (see 2 Kings 17).

12. TWO LEGS OR PIECE OF AN EAR: The Lord gives a vivid description of the small remnant left in Israel after the Assyrian invasion.

13. HEAR AND TESTIFY: As in verse 9, the heathen nations were once again called on to witness and testify of God's righteous judgment on Israel.

14. BETHEL: The principal location of idol worship in Israel (see 1 Kings 12:25–33).

*SIN OF IDOLATRY: Amos indicts Israel for idolatrous sacrifices and ritualistic religion, all of which were worthless to the Lord.*

4:1. COWS OF BASHAN: A deprecating description of the compassionless women of Samaria who lived luxurious lives (see Isaiah 3:16–26; 32:9–13; Jeremiah 4:30). Bashan was a fertile region below Mount Hermon east of the Jordan River and was known for its lush pastures. Under Jeroboam II, Israel was enjoying great prosperity.

2–3. THROUGH BROKEN WALLS . . . INTO HARMON: Captives will be mercilessly led out of the city through breaches in the walls, depicting massive overthrow. The location of Harmon is unknown.

2. HAS SWORN BY: See Amos 6:8; 8:7; see also Psalm 89:35; Isaiah 62:8; Jeremiah 44:26.

4. BETHEL . . . GILGAL: Bethel, the place of Jacob's dream (see Genesis 28), and Gilgal, where Israel was circumcised before surrounding Jericho (see Joshua 5:1–9), were sacred to Israel.

5. SACRIFICE OF THANKSGIVING WITH LEAVEN: Although prohibited from most offerings, leaven was required as a part of the thanksgiving offering (see Leviticus 7:11–15).

6–11. I GAVE YOU: Past warnings of famine, drought, crop failure, a plague, and military defeat were futile, a fact repeatedly emphasized by the statement, "Yet you have not returned to Me" (see verses 6, 8, 9, 10, 11).

6. CLEANNESS OF TEETH: The prophet Amos employed this euphemism to depict the absence of food during famine and drought sent by God to warn Israel, which he described in verses 6–9 (see also Deuteronomy 28:22–24, 47–48; Leviticus 26:18).

10. THE MANNER OF EGYPT: See Exodus 7–12.

11. FIREBRAND PLUCKED FROM THE BURNING: Only because of God's mercy was Israel saved from extinction (see Zechariah 3:2; Jude 1:23).

12. PREPARE TO MEET YOUR GOD: The general concept was first used of Israel's preparation to receive the covenant at Sinai (see Exodus 19:11, 15); here, she was implored to prepare for His judgment.

13. HE WHO FORMS MOUNTAINS: This is the God whom they were to be prepared to face. He is the Lord God Almighty who created, sustained, and is now ready to consume in judgment.

*SIN OF MORAL AND ETHICAL DECAY: Amos depicts a funeral dirge taken up for the nation of Israel for her sins, comparing her to a young woman who has died.*

5:3. HUNDRED LEFT . . . TEN LEFT: Most were to be killed in battle or taken captive (a ninety percent casualty vote); only a handful would return (see Amos 3:12; Isaiah 6:11–13).

5. BETHEL . . . GILGAL: See note on Amos 4:4.

BEERSHEBA: Located in southern Judah, fifty miles southwest of Jerusalem, Beersheba had a rich Israelite history (see Genesis 21:33; 26:23; 1 Samuel 8:1–3; 1 Kings 19:3–7). Apparently, people from the north crossed over the border to worship there (see 8:14).

6. HOUSE OF JOSEPH: This refers to the northern kingdom, since Ephraim and Manasseh, sons of Joseph, were two of its largest tribes.

7. JUSTICE TO WORMWOOD: Justice was so perverted that it was like wormwood, an herb known for its bitter taste (see Revelation 8:11).

8. PLEIADES AND ORION: Pleiades, part of the constellation Taurus, and Orion depict God's creative power and wisdom (see Job 9:9; 38:31–35). Israel was guilty of worshiping the stars (see Amos 5:26) instead of her Creator.

10–13. THEY HATE THE ONE: The fabric of justice had been destroyed, causing pervasive corruption "in the gates," the place where justice was administered (see verse 15; Deuteronomy 21:19; Joshua 20:4).

14–15. SEEK GOOD AND NOT EVIL: These were the righteous conditions necessary to turn back God's fast-approaching judgment.

16–17. THERE SHALL BE WAILING: Looking back at the previous accusations, Amos pictured the people mourning as the Lord passed through their midst, executing His sentence of judgment (see Exodus 11:3ff.). At the Exodus, the Lord "passed over" Israel; here, He "passes through," much like He did to the Egyptians in Moses's day.

18–20. WOE TO YOU WHO DESIRE THE DAY OF THE LORD: Even the wicked wanted the Day of the Lord to come, mistakenly thinking that it would bring victory/blessing instead of certain judgment (see Zephaniah 1:14–18).

21–24. I DESPISE YOUR FEAST DAYS: When performed with a corrupt heart (see Amos 4:4–5), even the "savored" festivals and offerings were despised by the Lord (see Leviticus 26:27, 31; Psalm 51:16–17, 19).

25–26. YOUR IDOLS . . . YOUR GODS: In addition to worshiping the Lord during the Exodus, Israel also worshiped other gods, carrying along "Sikkuth [or "tabernacle"] your king [or "Molech"] and Chiun, your idols." Molech worship included the astrological worship of Saturn and the host of heaven, plus the actual sacrificing of children (see 2 Kings 17:16–17). Warned against Molech worship (see Deuteronomy 18:9–13), Israel nevertheless pursued all facets of it, continuing with Solomon (see 1 Kings 11:7) and his descendants (see 1 Kings 12:28; 2 Kings 17:16–17; Jeremiah 32:35) until Josiah (see 2 Kings 23:10). Stephen recited Amos 5:25–27 when he recounted the past sins of Israel in Acts 7:42–43.

27. CAPTIVITY: Assyria conquered Damascus in 732 BC and then overtook Israel in 722 BC.

6:1–2. GO OVER: The two capitals of Judah and Israel, Zion (Jerusalem) and Samaria, were invited to look around. If Calneh (possibly the Calno of Isaiah 10:9) and Hamath (Syria) and Gath (Philistia) could not put off judgment, how could they?

3–8. WOE TO YOU: The Lord profiles the sinful and despicable lifestyle of the people whom He will judge.

6. DRINK WINE FROM BOWLS: These large bowls, usually used for sacrificial purposes, here typify the excesses of their lifestyle.

8. SWORN BY HIMSELF: See Amos 6:8; 8:7; Genesis 22:16; Isaiah 45:23; Jeremiah 49:13; 51:14; Hebrews 6:13–14.

9–10. TEN MEN REMAIN . . . SHALL DIE: The judgment was so comprehensive that even small remnants were sought out and killed.

10. ONE WHO WILL BURN: This could refer to cremation, demanded by the excessive number killed and the fear of epidemics. With rare exceptions (see 1 Samuel 31:12), corpses were buried in ancient Israel.

DARE NOT MENTION . . . THE LORD: Previously welcomed as a friend, the Lord came in judgment as a foe; survivors would not want to invoke His name out of fear.

12. DO HORSES RUN ON ROCKS: Israel's exercise of justice was as absurd as running horses on rocks or plowing rocks with oxen.

13. LO DEBAR . . . KARNAIM: Apparently, these were two Syrian sites captured by Jeroboam II (see 2 Kings 14:25). Lo Debar means "nothing" and sarcastically points out that Israel's "great" gain will amount to nothing. Karnaim means "horns," which symbolizes the strength of an animal. Israel foolishly believed they had conquered in their own strength.

14. A NATION: Assyria in 722 BC.

HAMATH TO THE VALLEY OF THE ARABAH: These represent the northern and southern perimeters of Israel as reestablished by Jeroboam II (see 2 Kings 14:25).

## UNLEASHING THE TEXT

1) What was the Lord communicating through His use of rhetorical questions in Amos 3:1–8?

_____

_____

_____

_____

_____

2) What can we learn from 4:6–13 about God's methods for catching our attention when we've wandered away from Him?

_____

_____

_____

_____

_____

_____

3) God called His people to repent in 5:4–15. What does it mean to "seek the LORD" when you are convicted regarding your sin?

_____

_____

_____

_____

_____

_____

4) What kind of imagery does the prophet Amos use in chapter 6? What do those images communicate?

_____

_____

_____

_____

_____

_____

## EXPLORING THE MEANING

**God cannot be ignored.** There is a curious grouping of rhetorical questions listed at the beginning of Amos 3, starting with, "Can two walk together, unless they are agreed?" (verse 3). The purpose of these questions was to show that some things in nature are certain. Lions do not roar when they have no prey. Snares do not spring up when nothing has triggered them. Trumpets are not blown in a city (an announcement of battle) without causing fear. In the same way, as Amos states in verse 7, God revealed His will to His people through the mouths of His prophets. The point of Amos's rhetorical method was to highlight the fact that Israel's leaders were attempting to ignore God's will by ignoring (and even silencing) His prophets. They were like children attempting to cover their ears in order to avoid hearing their parents' command to clean their rooms. But as verse 8 makes clear, God cannot be ignored: "A lion has roared! Who will not fear?" This was true during the time of the prophets, and it is still true today.

Some may think they have escaped God by avoiding church and avoiding Scripture, but they are only fooling themselves. God cannot be silenced.

*God cannot be bribed.* Amos was one of many prophets through whom God delivered His message of coming judgment and wrath. Ezekiel, Jeremiah, Hosea, and others prophesied about Israel's and Judah's destruction at the hands of foreign powers. So why did the people ignore these warnings? One reason seems to be that they believed their spiritual practices—their offerings, sacrifices, and rituals—would appease God's anger. This is why Amos 5:21 is so shocking: "I hate, I despise your feast days, and I do not savor your sacred assemblies." This was God speaking, and it was just the beginning: "Though you offer Me burnt offerings and your grain offerings, I will not accept them, nor will I regard your fattened peace offerings" (verse 22). The Israelites mistakenly believed they could use external actions to assuage their internal sinfulness. They tried to cover over their sins of their homes through pious activity in the temple. Their efforts failed. God made their fate clear: " 'Therefore I will send you into captivity beyond Damascus,' says the LORD, whose name is the God of hosts" (5:27).

*God's wrath cannot be avoided.* Few passages in Scripture are as scathing as God's rebuke against the "cows of Bashan" in Amos 4:1–5. This was a deprecating description of the compassionless women of Samaria who lived luxurious lives while oppressing the poor and crushing the needy. They were lovers of wine who gloried in immoralities of all kinds. God promised they would receive judgment for their sins: "Behold, the days shall come upon you when He will take you away with fishhooks, and your posterity with fishhooks" (verse 2). Similarly, Amos 6 describes prideful Israelites who "lie on beds of ivory, stretch out on your couches, eat lambs from the flock and calves from the midst of the stall" (verse 4). These people entertained themselves with wine, music, and frivolities yet were not "grieved for the affliction of Joseph" (verse 6). While many Israelites attempted to hide from God through their spiritual practices, these individuals tried to avoid God's wrath by standing behind their wealth and prestige. In their pride, they believed themselves to be above any consequences arising from their actions. They were wrong. In God's timing, He promised they would receive the just punishment for their callousness and their rebellion. This punishment came to pass when Assyria conquered the northern kingdom and took away the wealthy and poor alike into captivity.

## REFLECTING ON THE TEXT

5)   What are some ways our society tries to ignore God's presence and warnings?

6)   What safeguards have you put in place to ensure you are aware of God's presence in your life and His will for your life?

7)   What spiritual activities or disciplines have been important in your relationship with God? Where might you be in danger of focusing on those activities more than on God Himself?

8)   Where do you see similarities or areas of overlap between yourself and the objects of God's criticism in Amos 4 and 6?

## PERSONAL RESPONSE

9) The people of Israel failed to heed the many warnings delivered to them through God's prophets. Take a moment to assess your own life and lifestyle. What is one step you can take today to obey God's commands?

_____

_____

_____

_____

_____

_____

_____

10) Amos was faithful in delivering God's call to repentance. Where do you have an opportunity to speak truth to friends, loved ones, or even enemies, who are in rebellion against God?

_____

_____

_____

_____

_____

_____

_____

# 5

# VISIONS OF JUDGMENT
## *Amos 7:1 17*

## DRAWING NEAR

Imagine you had to deliver bad news to someone you love. How would you handle that task?

_____

_____

_____

_____

_____

_____

_____

_____

_____

_____

_____

## THE CONTEXT

So far in the text, Amos has delivered a series of prophecies concerning the future judgment of Israel's enemies (1:3–2:3) and the kingdom of Judah (2:4–5). He has also delivered a set of pronouncements against Israel, including condemnations for their sin of irresponsibility (3:1–15), their sin of idolatry (4:1–13), and their sin of moral/ethical decay (5:1–6:14). In doing so, Amos was declaring the word and will of God, thus fulfilling his role as a prophet.

Beginning in chapter 7, the text shifts to Amos's five prophetic visions. In the first vision, Amos sees a swarm of locusts devouring the people's portion of the harvest, after the king has received his share (7:1–3). In the second vision, Amos sees a fire that consumes the fields and causes the nation's water supply to dry up (7:4–6). But in each case, Amos cries out to the Lord for mercy, saying, "O Lord GOD, forgive, I pray! Oh, that Jacob may stand, for he is small!" (verse 2, see also verse 5). God relents from each judgment after listening to Amos's pleas.

In the third vision, the prophet Amos sees the Lord holding a plumb line (7:7–9). God tells Amos that He has measured the true spiritual nature of Israel and found her wanting—and this time, He does not relent from His judgment. The pronouncement leads into a "historical interlude" in which Amaziah, the priest of Bethel, accuses Amos of conspiracy against the king (7:10–17). The inclusion of this event is significant because it reveals that Israel's leaders—both political and religious—refused to acknowledge the word and will of God as spoken through His prophet.

## KEYS TO THE TEXT

Read Amos 7:1–17, noting the key words and phrases indicated below.

> *VISION OF FIRE, LOCUSTS, AND A PLUMB LINE: Amos describes the three visions that he received from the Lord. The first two depict the Lord's commitment to spare a remnant, while the last reveals the true spiritual nature of Israel.*

7:1–3. LOCUST SWARMS: The first vision, symbolizing God's action, pictured a swarm of locusts devouring the people's portion of the later cuttings, after the king had taken the first cutting (see Joel 1:2–12).

2. O LORD GOD, FORGIVE, I PRAY: Amos, so moved by seeing the potential devastation to Israel, interceded on their behalf, much like Moses had done in earlier times (see Exodus 32:30–32).

3. THE LORD RELENTED: God relented like He did at Abraham's pleading over Sodom in Genesis 18:22–23.

4–6. CONFLICT BY FIRE: Under the figure of fire, the second vision concerns a devastating drought, causing the underground water supplies to dry up and the fields to be consumed (see Deuteronomy 32:22). Amos again mercifully pleaded Israel's cause (see verses 2–3).

7–9. A PLUMB LINE IN HIS HAND: The true spiritual nature of Israel was here tested (and found wanting) by God's plumb line of righteousness in this third of five visions. The sword of judgment was to come from Assyria.

> AMAZIAH'S COMPLAINT: *The words of Amos cut deep into the heart of Israel's leadership, causing them to accuse him of conspiracy against the king.*

10. BETHEL: Remember that Bethel was the principal location of idol worship in Israel (see 1 Kings 12:25–33).

11. AMOS HAS SAID: This most likely refers to verse 9. Amaziah understood the Lord's message through Amos, but he rejected it.

12. GO . . . FLEE: Amos was being sent back home to Tekoa.

14–16. NO PROPHET . . . WORD OF THE LORD: Amos declares that he was a farmer by occupation but that God had spoken through him and Israel desperately needed to listen.

17. LED AWAY CAPTIVE: To Assyria, c. 722 BC.

## UNLEASHING THE TEXT

1) What images are most surprising in Amos 7? Why did these stand out to you?

_____

_____

_____

_____

_____

_____

_____

2) What do verses 1–6 say about God's desire to relent from passing judgment?

_____

_____

_____

_____

_____

_____

3) The "plumb line" referenced in verses 7–9 is a measuring tool that evaluates straightness. What are some spiritual indicators that help you evaluate yourself according to God's standards?

_____

_____

_____

_____

4) Look again at the historical interlude in verses 10–17. What was Amos risking by declaring the word of God to the leaders of Israel?

_____

_____

_____

_____

## EXPLORING THE MEANING

**God hears the prayers of His people.** Amos spoke of two visions he received from the Lord in 7:1–6. In the first vision, he saw a swarm of locusts devastating the crops of Israel. In the second vision, Amos saw God calling for "conflict by fire" that "consumed" (verse 4) much of Israel's territory. Both times Amos received those visions, he responded by crying out to God and interceding on behalf of the people. He asked God to "forgive" and "cease" His judgments, and in both cases, he concluded his prayer with this supplication: "Oh, that Jacob may stand, for he is small!" (verses 2, 5). And in both cases, God responded by relenting from His wrath and stating, "It shall not be" (verse 3). What do we learn from these visions? First and foremost, that God hears the prayers of His people. As the apostle John wrote, "Now this is the confidence that we have in Him, that if we ask anything according to His will, He hears us" (1 John 5:14). God not only hears our prayers but also responds to them in accordance with His sovereign will.

**God judges the rebellion of His people.** The first two of Amos's visions offered good news for the people of Israel. The third, however, did not. In that vision, Amos saw the Lord standing on a wall and holding a plumb line. This basic tool is essentially a weight tied to the end of a string. By holding the string high and keeping the weight off the ground, a worker can use the straightness of the string to measure or assess the straightness of his building materials. In Amos's vision, God used His plumb line to measure the "straightness" of Israel's actions—specifically, whether the actions of His people conformed to the standard of His Word. Not surprisingly, the Israelites were found wanting. They had continually rebelled against God's law and refused to heed His calls for repentance. As a result, God once again promised to judge that rebellion by allowing Assyria to invade and destroy the northern kingdom of Israel. God proclaimed, "The high places of Isaac shall be desolate, and the sanctuaries of Israel shall be laid waste. I will rise with the sword against the house of Jeroboam" (verse 9).

***God expects His servants to speak the truth.*** As mentioned above, Amos 7:10–17 contains a historical interlude in which Amaziah, Israel's leading priest, responded to Amos's prophetic declarations by complaining to Jeroboam II, the king of Israel. What is interesting is that Amaziah faithfully summarized the core message of Amos's prophecy: "For thus Amos has said: 'Jeroboam shall die by the sword, and Israel shall surely be led away captive from their own land' " (verse 11). In other words, Amaziah understood what God had communicated through Amos. He correctly perceived that God had promised to pour out judgment and wrath on the people of Israel. But Amaziah did not want to hear the truth, and even more critically, he did not want the rest of Israel's population to hear the truth. Therefore, he threatened Amos and tried to expel him from Bethel altogether. This is a critical reminder that God expects His servants to speak the truth, even when doing so is unpopular—and even dangerous. In the words of the apostle Paul, "Therefore, putting away lying, 'Let each one of you speak truth with his neighbor,' for we are members of one another" (Ephesians 4:25).

## REFLECTING ON THE TEXT

5) When has God answered your prayers? Did He answer those prayers in a way that was unexpected to you?

_____

_____

_____

_____

_____

_____

6) What is the appropriate response when it seems God is not hearing your prayers?

_____

_____

_____

_____

7) Based on what you know of God's expectations for followers of Christ, what are you doing well in your spiritual life? What sins remain that need to be killed?

_____

_____

_____

_____

8) What are some situations or circumstances in which it can be uncomfortable to speak the truth of Scripture to others? Why is this the case?

_____

_____

_____

_____

## PERSONAL RESPONSE

9) Think again about those moments when you feel uncomfortable standing for the truth of God's Word. What is one step you can take this week to express your faith in Scripture?

_____

_____

_____

_____

10) Take a moment to reflect on your sins based on God's "plumb line." Who might help you improve those areas of weakness? How can you seek that assistance?

_____

_____

_____

_____

# 6

# THE LORD WILL RESTORE
## Amos 8:1–9:15

## DRAWING NEAR

Imagine you had the resources to totally renovate your home. What would need to be torn down before you could begin the rebuilding process?

_____

_____

_____

_____

_____

_____

_____

_____

_____

_____

## THE CONTEXT

Amos 7 ended with a historical interlude in which Amaziah, the priest of Bethel, attempted to silence God's prophet and send him back to his hometown of Tekoa. However, Amos refused to be silenced. He told Amaziah that he was "no prophet" nor a "son of a prophet" but was a "sheepbreeder and a tender of sycamore fruit" (verse 14). In other words, Amos declared that he was a prophet by divine calling and had no ulterior motive than to warn God's people of coming judgment, and he again pleaded with them to listen to the warnings of the Lord.

As we saw in the previous lesson, the outburst from Amaziah occurred after Amos described a vision of God holding a plumb line and proclaiming that Israel had continually failed to measure up to the standard of His law. This was the third vision that Amos described in the chapter. The first two—a vision of locusts and a vision of fire—were each met with the prophet's plea for divine mercy and God relenting from enacting the judgment. But in the third vision, God declared that Israel's high places would be laid desolate, and her sanctuaries would be laid waste, and the sword would come against the house of her king.

In Amos 8–9, the prophet will relate the final two visions: a vision of summer fruit, and a vision of the Lord Himself. These passages confirm God's plan to pour out His wrath on Israel. Yet the book ends on a more hopeful note—with God's promise to again restore His people.

## Keys to the Text

Read Amos 8:1–9:15, noting the key words and phrases indicated below.

> VISION OF THE FRUIT BASKET: *In this fourth vision, God proclaims that just as fruit was fully ripened by the summer's sun, so Israel was ripe for His judgment.*

8:5. NEW MOON: Based on a lunar calendar, Israel would celebrate the day with a festival. Like the Sabbath, no work was to be done on this day (see 1 Samuel 20:5, 6; 2 Kings 4:23; Ezekiel 46:3). The merchants' eagerness for the day to end revealed their appetite for greed.

EPHAH SMALL . . . SHEKEL LARGE: By dishonest weighing, the merchant decreased the actual amount received and inflated the apparent cost of the misweighed merchandise. God detests dishonesty (see Leviticus 19:35–36; Deuteronomy 25:13–16; Ezekiel 45:10; Micah 6:10).

6. BAD WHEAT: This denotes the chaff, which was mixed into the good wheat to cheat the buyer.

7. PRIDE OF JACOB: As surely as the nation was filled with sinful pride (see Hosea 5:5; 7:10), so the Lord, who should have been "the Pride of Jacob" (Micah 5:4), would not forget her heinous works (see Amos 6:8). This is a play on words in which the Hebrew word for the worst of human pride is the same for the greatest of God's majesty. What the Lord detests in Israel (6:8), He will swear by in Himself.

8. HEAVE AND SUBSIDE LIKE THE RIVER OF EGYPT: Like the Nile River, which annually provided water and rich soil deposits for farmers by greatly overflowing its banks, so judgment would overflow the land of Israel for the unrighteous arrogance of the nation.

9. THE SUN GO DOWN AT NOON: This probably brings to mind the total eclipse of the sun c. 763 BC as a picture of God's coming judgment. The darkness will symbolize their mourning and actually increase it.

10. SACKCLOTH: Fabric generally made of goat's hair, usually black or dark in color (see Revelation 6:12), and usually placed on the bare body around the hips (see Genesis 37:34; 1 Kings 21:27), leaving the chest free for "beating" (see Isaiah 32:11–12). Sackcloth was used in the ancient world to depict sorrow and penitence (see Nehemiah 9:1; Isaiah 37:1; Matthew 11:21). Because the prophets' message usually dealt with a call to repentance, it became the principal garment worn by prophets (see Matthew 3:4; Revelation 11:3). This detailed picture of a mourning nation as depicted in Amos's prophecy is similar to the residents of Babylon mourning her ultimate demise (see Revelation 18:9–19).

11–12. FAMINE . . . OF HEARING THE WORDS OF THE LORD: During prosperity, the nation rejected the prophets (see Amos 7:10–17); in captivity, no word from the Lord could be found (see 1 Samuel 28:6ff.). What they once had in abundance and had rejected, they now desperately wanted but could not find, no matter how far they searched.

14. SAMARIA . . . DAN: Jeroboam I (931–910 BC) had built altars at both locations in an effort to keep Israel from going to Jerusalem to worship (see 1 Kings 12:26–29).

BEERSHEBA: See note on Amos 5:5. Their idolatrous practices will be eliminated permanently (see 5:2).

VISION OF THE ALTAR: *The fifth vision opens with the Lord standing beside the altar in Bethel, commanding that the temple be torn down, thus falling upon the worshipers. He would spare none (see Amos 5:2; 8:14).*

9:2–4. IT SHALL SLAY THEM: Desperate to escape, none can hide from the hand of judgment. Righteous David found solace in the omnipresence of God (see Psalm 139:7–10; Jeremiah 23:23–24); the wicked find only His wrath (see Revelation 20:13).

3. CARMEL: A mountainous region, rising 1,800 feet above the Mediterranean Sea, known for its many caves and forests. See note on Amos 1:2.

4. MY EYES: This is a figure of speech in reference to God's omniscience (see verse 8).

5–9. HE WHO TOUCHES THE EARTH: Lest people question the Lord's power, they are reminded of His omnipotence revealed in creation and in His sovereign rulership of the nations. Other nations have been transplanted from their homelands; why not Israel?

5. THE RIVER: See note on Amos 8:8.

7. CAPHTOR: The island of Crete.

KIR: See note on Amos 1:5.

8. EYES . . . LORD: See note on verse 4.

8–9. I WILL DESTROY IT FROM THE FACE OF THE EARTH: The northern kingdom of Israel would no longer exist after being destroyed by the Assyrians in 722 BC (see 2 Kings 17). However, God would preserve a remnant of Jacob's offspring to populate a bigger, better kingdom which He promised long ago to Abraham, Isaac, and Jacob.

9. SIFT . . . AMONG ALL NATIONS: Only the chaff was to be punished; God's remnant was to be preserved to inherit the blessings spoken of in the following verses.

> THE LORD WILL RESTORE: *Millennial blessings await the final faithful remnant, when Messiah personally reigns over all nations in Jerusalem on the throne of David, and the Jews are never again pulled up from their divinely inherited land.*

11. TABERNACLE OF DAVID: A reference to the dynasty of David. The promises of God in the Davidic covenant are alluded to here (see 2 Samuel 7:1–17). God will "raise up" and "rebuild" this tabernacle on earth for Christ to rule in His millennial kingdom (see Zechariah 14:9–11). The apostles used this passage to illustrate that Gentiles could thus be a part of God's redemption.

13–14. PLOWMAN . . . GRAPES . . . MOUNTAINS . . . HILLS: Prosperity, in hyperbolic terms, is here described (see Leviticus 26:5; Joel 3:18; contrast Isaiah 5). Fruitfulness is so enormous that planting and reaping seasons overlap. This prosperity will encourage massive repatriation (see Isaiah 11:15–16) and reconstruction (see Zechariah 2:1–5).

15. NO LONGER SHALL THEY BE PULLED UP FROM THE LAND: The ultimate fulfillment of God's land promise to Abraham (see Genesis 12:7; 15:7; 17:8) will occur during Christ's millennial reign on earth (see Joel 2:26–27).

## UNLEASHING THE TEXT

1) What is the message of Amos's fourth vision (summer fruit) in 8:1–14?

_____

_____

_____

_____

_____

2) What are the similarities between the culture of Israel in Amos's day and our culture today?

_____

_____

_____

_____

_____

_____

3) What images stood out in Amos's fifth vision (vision of the Lord) in 9:1–10?

_____

_____

_____

_____

_____

_____

4) What specific promises did God make concerning the people in 9:11–15?

_____

_____

_____

_____

_____

## EXPLORING THE MEANING

**God hates injustice.** On one level, Amos's vision of the basket of summer fruit is simple to understand. Just as fruit becomes ripened by the sun during the summer season, so Israel had become ripe for judgment after decades of rebellion against God. Amos made it evident that God's judgment would be carried out soon. But at another level, the vision is complex when we explore the many details that God provided regarding Israel's sin. Those details are found in 8:4–14, and they paint the picture of a nation founded on injustice. The Israelites swallowed up the needy and made the poor to fall (see verse 4). Their merchants brushed off the importance of religious festivals and Sabbaths, wanting only to reopen their shops and make more money (see verse 5). The children of Israel were swollen with pride. Though they had received warnings from God regarding their doom, they ignored them all. As a result, they would endure not only destruction and captivity but also silence from heaven (see verses 11–12). God's hatred for injustice was not isolated to the ancient Israelites . . . it is part of His character. As we read in Proverbs, "He who justifies the wicked, and he who condemns the just, both of them alike are an abomination to the LORD" (17:15).

**God is able to tear down what is broken.** Amos 9 begins with a visual that describes the prophet's fifth and final vision: God destroying the altar at Bethel. "I saw the Lord standing by the altar, and He said: 'Strike the doorposts, that the thresholds may shake, and break them on the heads of them all. I will slay the last of them with the sword" (verse 1). This vision recalls the final moments of Samson's life, when he stood between the pillars of the false god Dagon and—with strength from the Holy Spirit—brought the temple down to kill thousands of enemy Philistines (see Judges 16). In Amos's vision, it is God who strikes the doorposts of the altar at Bethel and brings it down upon the Israelites. This altar had been set up by Jeroboam II (c. 793–753 BC) to prevent his subjects in the northern kingdom of Israel from traveling down to Jerusalem to worship God at His temple (see 1 Kings 12:25–29), so it was a source of idolatry from the beginning. God had been patient for generations, faithfully calling His people to repentance. In the end, however, an idolatrous people would not be reformed. What was broken needed to be torn down, and God was able to do so in His sovereignty.

**God can rebuild what seems lost.** The vision of God destroying the altar at Bethel offered a foreshadowing of the destruction on the horizon for the entire northern kingdom of Israel. The Assyrians not only destroyed Bethel in 722 BC but also put thousands of Israelites to the sword and carried the rest away into captivity. For those Israelites, it seemed that God's promises of a homeland for His people were lost beyond repair. Yet the final verses of Amos strike a more hopeful tone: "On that day I will raise up the tabernacle of David, which has fallen down, and repair its damages; I will raise up its ruins, and rebuild it as in the days of old" (9:11). No longer focused on the altar at Bethel, God instead spoke of "the tabernacle of David." This was a reference to God's promise in 2 Samuel 7 that He would build David a "house" that would stand forever. That house was David's dynasty, which culminated in the Messiah, Jesus Christ. As part of that promise, God also declared, "Moreover I will appoint a place for My people Israel, and will plant them, that they may dwell in a place of their own and move no more; nor shall the sons of wickedness oppress them anymore" (2 Samuel 7:10). This promise seemed lost for the people of Israel when Assyria invaded their land—and later for the people of Judah when Babylon destroyed Jerusalem. Yet the final verses of Amos point forward to the ultimate fulfillment of God's promises to His people: " 'I will plant them in their land, and no longer shall they be pulled up from the land I have given them,' says the LORD your God" (9:15).

## REFLECTING ON THE TEXT

5) How does the Bible define injustice? What are some examples of it in our culture today?

_____

_____

_____

_____

_____

_____

6) The Israelites were ripe for judgment because of their rebellion against God. What features of our culture evidence a similar rejection of God and His Word?

_____

_____

_____

_____

_____

7)  On a personal level, what does it look like for God to expose your sin?

_____
_____
_____
_____
_____
_____

8)  Do you meditate on your true home in heaven? How does that mindset help you live faithfully on earth?

_____
_____
_____
_____
_____
_____

## Personal Response

9)  Spend a few minutes in prayer, asking the Holy Spirit to reveal any sins in your life that need to be put to death. Write down what He brings to mind.

_____
_____
_____
_____
_____
_____

10) What would you like God to build or achieve in your life within the coming year? What vision are you pressing toward as His child?

_____
_____
_____
_____
_____
_____

# 7

# HOSEA AND GOMER

## Hosea 1:1–3:5

## DRAWING NEAR

Who has been a positive example of a productive marriage in your life? What lessons have you learned from observing that couple?

_____

_____

_____

_____

_____

_____

_____

_____

_____

_____

## THE CONTEXT

There are a number of wonderful love stories recorded in Scripture, beginning, of course, with Adam and Eve (see Genesis 2–3). Other notable examples include Isaac and Rebekah (see Genesis 24), Jacob and Rachel (Genesis 29), Ruth and Boaz (see Ruth 2–4), Solomon and his Shulamite bride (see Song of Solomon 1–8), and Mary and Joseph (see Matthew 1). These stories in the pages of the Bible affirm the value of romantic love and marital partnership.

The story of Hosea and Gomer could be included in that list—although the circumstances surrounding their relationship are more mysterious (and more tragic). As noted in the Introduction, Hosea served as the Lord's prophet faithfully for decades, prophesying during the reigns of Uzziah (790–739 BC), Jotham (750–731 BC), Ahaz (735–715 BC), and Hezekiah (715–686 BC) in Judah, and Jeroboam II (793–753 BC) and the last six kings from Zechariah (753–752 BC) to Hoshea (732–722 BC) in Israel. He declared the word of God to the people of Israel and to her kings. However, he is best known for his up-and-down marriage to Gomer.

In the opening chapter of Hosea, the prophet describes how God commanded him to marry this woman who would be unfaithful to him (see Hosea 1:2). Later, the Lord would command him to pursue his wife even after her unfaithfulness and restore their relationship (see 3:1). In doing so, Hosea created a wonderful picture of God's love for faithless Israel.

## KEYS TO THE TEXT

Read Hosea 1:1–3:5, noting the key words and phrases indicated below.

> HOSEA'S UNFAITHFUL WIFE: *The word of the Lord comes to the prophet Hosea and instructs him to "take yourself a wife of harlotry and children of harlotry" (Hosea 1:2).*

1:1. THE WORD OF THE LORD: This kind of introduction, expressing the prophet's divine authority and message source, appears also in Joel 1:1, Micah 1:1, Zephaniah 1:1, Zechariah 1:1, and Malachi 1:1. Similar statements appear in Amos 1:3, Obadiah 1, Jonah 1:1, and Haggai 1:2.

2. CHILDREN OF HARLOTRY: This points to the future unfaithfulness of their mother. The children were possibly not fathered by Hosea. That Hosea's marriage to Gomer was to depict God's marriage to Israel is clearly set forth and becomes the key to the theme of the book.

4. JEZREEL: Meaning "God will scatter" (see Zechariah 10:9), the name is given to the child so named as a prediction of judgment (see 2 Kings 9:7–10:28).

I WILL AVENGE THE BLOODSHED OF JEZREEL: It was at the city of Jezreel where Jehu slaughtered the house of Ahab (see 2 Kings 9:7–10:28).

BRING AN END: This looks forward to the exile of Israel to Assyria in 722 BC, from which she never returned.

5. THE VALLEY OF JEZREEL: Jezreel, called Esdraelon, extends ten miles in breadth from the Jordan River to the Mediterranean Sea, near Carmel; it was the great battlefield (see Revelation 16:14–16) adjoining the Valley of Megiddo, which will become an avenue of blessing (see Hosea 1:11) when Christ returns in triumph.

BREAK THE BOW: The bow was a common euphemism denoting military strength, the principal instrument of warfare in Israel. Fulfillment came in 722 BC when Assyria invaded.

6. LO-RUHAMAH: Literally, "not pitied," this daughter is named to symbolize God bringing judgment on Israel, no longer extending His favor toward them (see 1 Peter 2:10).

7. I WILL HAVE MERCY ON . . . JUDAH: God chose to intervene on behalf of Hezekiah when Jerusalem was besieged at the hands of the Assyrians in 701 BC (see 2 Kings 19; Isaiah 37).

9. LO-AMMI: The name means "not My people" and symbolizes God's rejection of Israel.

I WILL NOT BE YOUR GOD: Literally, "I will not be 'I am' to you." The phrase gives the breaking of the covenant, a kind of divorce formula, in contrast to the covenant or marriage formula, "I am that I am," given in Exodus 3:14.

*RESTORATION OF ISRAEL: In spite of the waywardness of Israel, God will preserve a future remnant for Himself from both Israel and Judah.*

10–11: AS THE SAND OF THE SEA: To this remnant that God preserves from Israel and Judah, the Lord will say *Ammi* (1:9) and show *Ruhamah* (1:6; see 1 Peter 2:10). Speaking of millennial blessings, God promised national increase (see Isaiah 54:1), national conversion and reunion (see Ezekiel 37:15–23), national leadership (see Hosea 3:5), and national restoration (see 2:23).

NUMBER: A reaffirmation of the Abrahamic covenant, not to be fulfilled in this generation, but in the future (see Genesis 22:17).

NOT MY PEOPLE: Quoted by Paul in Romans 9:26.

11. ONE HEAD: This refers to Messiah (see Hosea 3:5).

DAY OF JEZREEL: Here, used positively in the sense of divine blessing (see Hosea 2:22), in contrast to the idea of scattering in judgment (see 1:4).

2:2. BRING CHARGES AGAINST YOUR MOTHER: Although the language is applicable to Gomer, it depicts a courtroom scene in which the Lord, as the plaintiff, brings charges against the defendant. Individual Israelites, depicted as the children, are commanded to bring charges against their mother, Israel, as a nation. The physical immorality of Gomer pictures the spiritual idolatry of Israel.

5. I WILL GO: Literally, "Let me go," it denotes strong desire and bent. Israel attributed her prosperity to the idols of her heathen neighbors, "her lovers" (see verses 7, 10, 12). She would not be deterred from pursuing them.

8–13. SHE DID NOT KNOW: The Lord withheld rain and productivity to show Israel that the Canaanite god Baal was not the god of rain and fertility—and not even a god.

8. PREPARED FOR BAAL: See Hosea 13:1. The worship of Baal (the Phoenician sun god), already present during the time of the judges (see Judges 2:17; 3:3; 8:33), became established in Israel when king Ahab married Jezebel, who attempted to obliterate Israelite worship of the true God (see 1 Kings 19). Offerings to Baal actually came from God's dowry to Israel (see Ezekiel 16:10–14).

10. I WILL UNCOVER HER LEWDNESS: God pledged to expose Israel's wickedness. The phrase is linked to being taken forcibly into captivity in Ezekiel 16:37–40.

HER LOVERS: The idols were personified as if they could see, though they could offer no help.

11. FEAST DAYS: Ever since the Exodus from Egypt, Israel had intermingled the worship of the Lord with the worship of false gods (see Amos 5:26; Acts 7:43).

13. BUT ME SHE FORGOT: See 2 Kings 17:7–18 for a detailed description of what the people's abandonment of God involved.

14. SPEAK COMFORT TO HER: The phrase was used of wooing (Genesis 34:3; Judges 19:3; Ruth 2:13). God will restore Israel to Himself.

15. VALLEY OF ACHOR: Literally, "Valley of Trouble," near Jericho where Achan and his family were judged (see Joshua 7:24). This promise alerts Israel that her discipline and judgment would not last forever because there is a "door of hope."

16. MY HUSBAND . . . MY MASTER: The former term (literally, "my *ishi*") denotes affection and intimacy, while the latter term (literally, "my *baali*") speaks of rulership.

17. REMEMBERED . . . NO MORE: In verse 13, Israel forgot her true God; here God said she would forget her false gods. What the outward conformity to the Mosaic covenant could not do, God does through a new, regenerated heart in the New Covenant (see Jeremiah 31:31–34; Zechariah 13:1–2).

18. A COVENANT: This depicts a millennial scene (see Isaiah 2:4; 11:6–9; Micah 4:3) when God's people become subject to God and creation becomes subject to them.

19–20. I WILL BETROTH YOU: Repeated three times, the term emphasizes the intensity of God's restoring love for the nation. In that day, Israel will no longer be thought of as a prostitute. Israel brings nothing to the marriage; God makes all the promises and provides all the dowry. These verses are recited by every orthodox Jew as he places the phylacteries on his hand and forehead (see Deuteronomy 11:18). The regeneration/conversion of the nation is much like that of an individual (see 2 Corinthians 5:16–19).

21–23. I WILL ANSWER: A dramatic reversal of circumstances (compare Hosea 1:4, 6, 9 with 1:10–2:1).

22. JEZREEL: Literally, "God will scatter." As in Hosea 1:11, it is used here in the positive sense of scattering seed to sow it.

23. NOT MY PEOPLE . . . ARE MY PEOPLE: Quoted by Paul in Romans 9:25.

*BOTH PARTIES RECONCILED: Having been previously separated, Hosea was commanded to pursue his estranged wife Gomer, thereby illustrating God's unquenchable love for faithless Israel.*

3:1. RAISIN CAKES: Eaten as a part of special occasions (see 2 Samuel 6:19), they may have been used in idolatrous ceremonies, possibly as an aphrodisiac (see Song of Solomon 2:5).

2. BOUGHT HER: Probably from a slave auction. Hosea purchased Gomer for fifteen shekels of silver and one and one-half homers of barley. Together, the total value may have equaled thirty pieces of silver, the price paid for a common slave (see Exodus 21:32). Barley was the offering of a person accused of adultery (see Numbers 5:15).

3–5. NOR SHALL YOU HAVE A MAN: Gomer would not be allowed conjugal relations for "many days" with any man, including Hosea. As a further element of the picture of God's dealings with His covenant people during the present age, Israel would exist without her existing political and religious (both true and false) relations until Messiah returns at the Second Advent to set up His millennial reign (see Ezekiel 40–48; Zechariah 12–14).

4. WITHOUT EPHOD OR TERAPHIM: Idolatrous items of priestly clothing and objects of worship.

5. DAVID: See Hosea 1:11. This must refer to Messiah during the Millennium, as "in the latter days" specifies (see Isaiah 55:3, 4; Jeremiah 30:9; Ezekiel 34:23–24; 37:24–25). The Jews did not seek after Christ at His First Advent. This reference has the Davidic covenant as its background (see 2 Samuel 7:12–17; Psalms 39; 132).

## UNLEASHING THE TEXT

1) What does chapter 1 convey about Hosea?

_____

_____

_____

_____

_____

2) What was God communicating through the names of Hosea's children?

_____

_____

_____

_____

_____

3) What is the evidence of God's love for Israel throughout Hosea 2?

_____

_____

_____

_____

_____

4) The text uses Gomer's infidelity as an illustration of Israel's idolatry and unfaithfulness to God. What are some ways modern followers of Jesus drift toward spiritual infidelity?

_____

_____

_____

_____

_____

## EXPLORING THE MEANING

*We are called to be faithful to God.* The marriage between Hosea and Gomer served as an illustration of the relationship between God and His people. But Hosea's marriage was not a metaphor; he took Gomer as his wife, and the text seems to indicate that he desired her to be faithful to him—and to their children. In the same way that Hosea expected faithfulness from Gomer, so God expected faithfulness from the Israelites. The connection between God and His people was also not a metaphor. God had entered into a covenant with Abraham's descendants—similar to a marriage covenant—in which He said, "I will take you as My people, and I will be your God" (Exodus 6:7). Followers of Jesus are also expected to maintain a spiritually faithful relationship with God. In fact, the New Testament uses similar imagery of the church as Christ's "bride." As Paul wrote, "Husbands, love your wives, just as Christ also loved the church and gave Himself for her, that He might sanctify and cleanse her with the washing of water by the word" (Ephesians 5:25–26). The book of Revelation uses this same terminology, stating, "Let us be glad and rejoice and give Him glory, for the marriage of the Lamb has come, and His wife has made herself ready" (19:7).

*We are unable to remain faithful to God.* Hosea 2 describes Israel's spiritual adultery, which was represented by Gomer's marital unfaithfulness. At times, God speaks of Israel in ways that seem stern and harsh. For example, He states, "Let her [Israel] put away her harlotries from her sight, and her adulteries from between her breasts; lest I strip her naked and expose her, as in the day she was born" (verse 2–3). He also says, "Now I will uncover her lewdness in the sight of her lovers, and no one shall deliver her from My hand" (verse 10). By using the language of a betrayed spouse, God was revealing the reality of Israel's unfaithfulness—and His love. Having entered into a covenant with the Israelites, God condemned their inability to keep that covenant. But even more, He rightly condemned their lack of desire to keep it. Christians today face a similar dilemma in that we are unable to remain perfectly faithful to Christ. Like Gomer, we wander, drift, and sin. As Paul lamented, "We know that the law is spiritual, but I am carnal, sold under sin. For what I am doing, I do not understand. For what I will to do, that I do not practice; but what I hate, that I do" (Romans 7:14–15).

*God's faithfulness overwhelms our faithlessness.* As mentioned above, all God's children are like Gomer in terms of our spiritual infidelity. We do not have the capacity to maintain our covenant relationship with Christ. This is the bad news. The good news is that God's love has swallowed up our infidelity through the death and resurrection of Christ. His faithfulness overwhelms our faithlessness. As Paul declared, "O wretched man that I am! Who will deliver me from this body of death? I thank God—through Jesus Christ our Lord!" (Romans 7:24–25). The primary message of Hosea and Gomer's marriage is not the unfaithfulness of Israel but the faithfulness of God. Listen to the tenderness in God's words to His people: " 'And it shall be, in that day,' says the LORD, 'that you will call Me "My Husband," and no longer call Me "My Master" ' " (2:16). And again: "Then I will say to those who were not My people, 'You are My people!' And they shall say, 'You are my God!' " (verse 23). In spite of our idolatry and our sinfulness, God is faithful in maintaining His love for us. He is, and always will be, faithful.

## REFLECTING ON THE TEXT

5)   What does it mean to be spiritually faithful as a child of God?

_____

_____

_____

_____

_____

_____

6)   How is infidelity an accurate analogy for our sin and rebellion?

_____

_____

_____

_____

_____

_____

7)   What still tempts you toward spiritual adultery? How do you respond?

_____

_____

_____

_____

8) God is always faithful to His promises—even when we're not. How is His faithfulness both a rebuke and an encouragement to you?

_____

_____

_____

_____

_____

_____

_____

## PERSONAL RESPONSE

9) What are some sinful habits in your life that keep causing you to ask, *Why am I doing this?* When do those habits seem to manifest most often?

_____

_____

_____

_____

_____

_____

_____

_____

10) What are some ways that God has proven Himself to be faithful to you? Use the space below to make a list, and be as specific as possible.

_____

_____

_____

_____

_____

_____

_____

_____

# 8

# ADULTEROUS ISRAEL
# FOUND GUILTY

*Hosea 4:1–6:3*

## DRAWING NEAR

When it comes to legal crimes, what are the mechanisms your community uses to determine guilt and innocence?

_____

_____

_____

_____

_____

_____

_____

_____

_____

_____

_____

_____

## THE CONTEXT

As we noted in the previous lesson, the first three chapters of Hosea largely focus on the prophet's marriage to a woman named Gomer. The Lord had commanded Hosea to take "a wife of harlotry" (Hosea 1:2), and she bore him two sons and a daughter. As God had foretold, Gomer was unfaithful to Hosea, representing Israel's spiritual unfaithfulness in its relationship with God. But then the Lord instructed Hosea to pursue his estranged wife and restore their relationship, thus symbolizing how God would restore His relationship with His people.

The theme of Israel's spiritual unfaithfulness continues in chapter 4 and throughout the rest of the book. However, the immediate focus moves away from Hosea's marriage. Instead, God instructs Hosea to bring a "charge" against the people of Israel. In this way, the chapter functions as a legal or judicial proclamation against God's people, declaring them guilty of idolatry. The latter half of the chapter specifically calls out the spiritual leaders who knew the expectations of their God yet still led their people toward "harlotry."

In chapter 5, the prophet details the impending consequences of that idolatry, including the nation's spiritual isolation and eventual exile—which, as we have seen, would occur when the Assyrian king Tiglath-Pileser captured Israel and forcibly relocated its people to its empire in 722 BC. But the first three verses of chapter 6 serve as a balm to this judicial indictment, revealing that Israel's future will be a time of healing and restoration.

## KEYS TO THE TEXT

Read Hosea 4:1–6:3, noting the key words and phrases indicated below.

> GOD'S CHARGE AGAINST ISRAEL: *Turning from the analogy of his own marriage, the prophet now makes the judicial charge in God's indictment against Israel.*

4:2. SWEARING . . . LYING . . . KILLING . . . STEALING . . . ADULTERY: Note the many infractions of the Ten Commandments (see Exodus 20:3–17).

3. THE LAND WILL MOURN: Sin plays havoc with humanity and nature (see Joel 1:17–20; Romans 8:19–22). In Zechariah 1:3, the prophet spoke of the fulfillment of the Day of the Lord, when even animal and physical creation will be affected by God's judgment of the earth.

4. LET NO MAN CONTEND: Rationalizing and denying their wrongs, the people protested their innocence, like those who would not humbly accept the decision of the priests (see Deuteronomy 17:8–13).

5. STUMBLE: Literally, "to totter," "to trip and fall," or "to stumble." The prophets frequently used this word to describe the spiritual life of the Hebrews.

For example, the prophet Hosea compares both false prophets and their followers to those who stumble in the dark—they are stumbling over the sin of idolatry and falling to their ruin (see Hosea 4:5; 5:5). The prophet Isaiah warns that those who rely on their own strength will stumble and fall (see Isaiah 40:30), but those who are led by the Lord will not stumble (see 63:13). In fact, the Lord will provide strength to those who have stumbled in the past and now call upon Him (see 1 Samuel 2:4).

YOUR MOTHER: The Israelite nation of which the people are the children (see Hosea 2:2).

6. REJECT YOU FROM BEING PRIEST FOR ME: Having rejected the Lord's instruction, Israel could no longer serve as His priest to the nations (see Exodus 19:6; James 3:1).

7–10. IT SHALL BE: LIKE PEOPLE, LIKE PRIEST: The priests' position of power and glory, abused in succeeding generations by the eating of the sin offerings, would be turned to shame. Being no different than the people, the priests, who should have been faithful, would share their punishment (see Isaiah 24:1–3). As it was in Hosea's time, so was it in Malachi's era almost four centuries later (see Malachi 2:1–9).

11. ENSLAVE THE HEART: Here is a moral truth applicable to all people and times, especially to Israel and Judah in Hosea's lifetime.

12. SPIRIT OF HARLOTRY: A prevailing mindset and inclination to worldly, spiritual immorality; i.e., idolatry (see Hosea 5:4).

13. SACRIFICES ON THE MOUNTAINTOPS: Bereft of righteous teaching and understanding, the people sacrificed to idols. Hilltops and groves of trees were favorite places for idolatrous worship (see Deuteronomy 12:2; Jeremiah 2:20; Ezekiel 6:13), including sinful religious prostitution.

14. THE MEN THEMSELVES GO APART WITH HARLOTS: Although all who sin will be judged, God forbade punishing the adulteresses alone and leaving the men who patronized them to go free. The heaviest punishment would not be on the women who sin but on the fathers and husbands who set such a bad example by their engagement with prostitutes.

DO NOT UNDERSTAND: see Hosea 4:6.

15. PLAY THE HARLOT: This refers to having illicit sexual relations, especially involving prostitution. Two forms of prostitution were practiced in the ancient world: (1) common prostitution, and (2) ritual or "religious" prostitution, which involved pagan fertility rites. Both forms were strictly forbidden

in God's law (see Leviticus 19:29; Deuteronomy 23:17). The Old Testament frequently uses prostitution as an image of the sin of idolatry. Israel was pledged to serve one God (Exodus 20:3), so idolatry was like marital unfaithfulness against the Lord. Hosea actually married a prostitute as a living symbol of God's patience with Israel's infidelities (1:2).

15. GILGAL: Between Jordan and Jericho in the area of Samaria, this was once a holy place to God (see Joshua 5:10–15; 1 Samuel 10:8; 15:21), afterward desecrated by idol worship (see Hosea 9:15; 12:11; see also Amos 4:4; 5:5).

BETH AVEN: Judah was to stay away from Israel's centers of false worship, including Beth Aven ("house of wickedness/deceit"). This was a deliberate substitution for the name Bethel ("house of God"), once sacred to God (see Genesis 28:17, 19), but made by Jeroboam a place to worship calves (see 1 Kings 12:28–33; 13:1; Jeremiah 48:13; Amos 3:14; 7:13).

16. ISRAEL IS STUBBORN: Because Israel was like a stubborn calf, God no longer attempted to corral her, abandoning her as a lamb in a vast wilderness.

17. EPHRAIM . . . LET HIM ALONE: As the largest and most influential of the ten northern tribes, Ephraim's name was often used as representative of the northern nation. This was an expression of God's wrath of abandonment. When sinners reject Him and are bent on fulfilling their wicked purposes, God removes restraining grace and turns them over to the results of their own perverse choices. This kind of wrath is that written about in Romans 1:18–32 (see also Judges 10:13; 2 Chronicles 15:2; 24:20; Psalm 81:11–12).

> *IMPENDING JUDGMENT ON ISRAEL AND JUDAH: Hosea addresses this next section to the priests, the people, and the royal family; the three imperatives demand attention.*

5:1. YOU HAVE BEEN A SNARE: The religious and civil leaders had entrapped the people (see Hosea 6:9; 7:7).

MIZPAH . . . TABOR: Mizpah of Gilead, lying east of the Jordan River (see Judges 10:17; 11:29), and Tabor, southwest of the Sea of Galilee, were likely places for false worship.

2–4. SLAUGHTER . . . HARLOTRY: The disobedient priests still slaughtered animals for unacceptable sacrifices rendered with sinful hearts to pagan gods.

5. PRIDE OF ISRAEL TESTIFIES TO HIS FACE: Israel's pride in idolatry provided self-incrimination (see Hosea 7:10).

JUDAH: This is the first of eleven indictments of the southern kingdom—the others are found in Hosea 5:10, 12, 13, 14; 6:4, 11; 8:14; 10:11; 11:12; 12:2—in a book that is primarily directed toward the northern kingdom.

6–7. WILL NOT FIND HIM: Israel's religious sacrifices and monthly festivals no longer brought divine favor, only judgment. God "has withdrawn Himself from them." See note on Hosea 4:17.

8. BLOW . . . HORN: The enemy was already upon them, and thus her watchmen were to sound the alarm (see Numbers 10:9).

GIBEAH . . . RAMAH: These cities were located on Judah's northern border with Israel.

BETH AVEN: Or Bethel, situated in southern Israel (see Hosea 4:15). All three were strategic defense cities.

BENJAMIN: This refers to the entire southern kingdom.

10. JUDAH: The southern kingdom was not innocent either.

REMOVE A LANDMARK: Boundaries, marked by stones, could be easily moved at night. Moving them was tantamount to stealing land from a neighbor (see Deuteronomy 19:14; 27:17; Proverbs 22:28; 23:10). Worse, Judah's leaders were moving spiritual lines established by God.

11. EPHRAIM IS OPPRESSED: Ephraim suffers for following man's will, not God's will.

12. MOTH . . . ROTTENNESS: God will be destructive to Israel.

13. KING JAREB: Jareb means "warrior" and refers to the king of Assyria (see Hosea 10:6), to whom Israel (see 2 Kings 15:19–20) and later Judah (see 2 Kings 16:5–9) turned for help.

14–15. NO ONE SHALL RESCUE: Foreign assistance would be of no value, since the Lord was orchestrating lion-like punishment (see Hosea 13:7–8) at the hands of the Assyrians for Israel and the Babylonians for Judah. He would remove Himself "till they acknowledge their offense" and "seek My face" (see also Hosea 3:5).

6:1–3. COME, AND LET US RETURN TO THE LORD: Coming with the beginning of Christ's millennial reign (see Zechariah 12:10–13:1; Isaiah 43:1–6), Hosea records Israel's future words of repentance (see also Hosea 5:15).

2. AFTER TWO DAYS . . . ON THE THIRD DAY: This is not a reference to the resurrection of Christ (illness, not death, is in the context of verse 1), but to the quickness of healing and restoration. Numbers are used similarly for literary effect elsewhere (e.g., Job 5:19; Proverbs 6:16; 30:15, 18; Amos 1:3).

## UNLEASHING THE TEXT

1) What are some of the ways the people of Israel had broken the basic tenets of the Ten Commandments according to Hosea 4:1–2?

_____

_____

_____

_____

_____

_____

2) What did God specially say about Israel's "harlotry" in 4:11–13?

_____

_____

_____

_____

_____

_____

3) What consequences did God declare for the Israelites in chapter 5?

_____

_____

_____

_____

_____

4) Read Hosea 6:1–3 again. What does it mean for an individual to repent of spiritual unfaithfulness? What would it mean for Israel to "return" to the Lord?

_____

_____

_____

_____

_____

_____

## EXPLORING THE MEANING

*Idolatry is foolish.* One of the main complaints in God's charge against Israel was that their idolatry had pushed them toward all manner of evil practices within the community. Hosea mentioned swearing, lying, killing, stealing, adultery, bloodshed, and more (see 4:2). Such practices were an abomination within a society that was supposed to reflect the character of God. But Hosea also took pains to show the foolishness of Israel's idolatry: "My people ask counsel from their wooden idols, and their staff informs them" (verse 12). In the context of God's legal charge against Israel, the image expressed here is of the Israelite leaders trying to seek advice or instruction from wooden carvings and attempting to engage their walking sticks in meaningful conversation. This theme echoes the words of Isaiah's famous rebuke of idolatry in Isaiah 44, where the prophet described a craftsman who found a piece of wood and used half of it to cook a meal over a fire. As for the second half: "The rest of it he makes into a god, his carved image. He falls down before it and worships it, prays to it and says, 'Deliver me, for you are my god!'" (44:17). In every context, including our own, idolatry is a foolish practice.

*Idolatry separates us from God.* Choosing to worship something created by human hands is silly on a practical level, but it is also deeply destructive on a spiritual level because idolatry causes separation from God. Hosea described that separation multiple times in chapters 4 and 5: "For Israel is stubborn like a stubborn calf; now the LORD will let them forage like a lamb in open country" (4:16); "Ephraim is joined to idols, let him alone" (verse 17); "With their flocks and herds they shall go to seek the LORD, but they will not find Him; He has withdrawn Himself from them" (5:6). It is important to remember this separation is a consequence of all forms of idolatry; it is not limited to the worship of physical objects. When believers today choose to pursue anything ahead of God—whether that is money, affection, achievement, approval, physical health, or anything else—they drift into idolatry, and the result is spiritual chaos. In the words of the apostle Paul, "Therefore, my beloved, flee from idolatry" (1 Corinthians 10:14).

*Idolatry can be rejected.* After two chapters detailing the Lord's judicial charge against Israel and the coming consequences for their unfaithfulness, the beginning verses of Hosea 6 offer a ray of hope, including this line: "Come, and let us return to the LORD; for He has torn, but He will heal us; He has stricken, but

He will bind us up" (verse 1). In the context of Hosea's prophecy, these verses point to Israel's restoration during the Millennial Kingdom of Christ. Israel's repentance and restoration has not yet taken place—nor will it occur until Christ's Millennial reign as described in Revelation 19–20—but even so, Hosea's words reflect the important biblical principle that idolatry can be rejected and our relationship with God restored. Spiritual unfaithfulness causes separation from God, but that distance can be removed through repentance. The Lord offered this promise of restoration to the Israelites on many occasions, saying, "If My people who are called by My name will humble themselves, and pray and seek My face, and turn from their wicked ways, then I will hear from heaven, and will forgive their sin and heal their land" (2 Chronicles 7:14). The Lord has also extended this promise to disciples of Jesus in the New Testament, saying to us, "If we confess our sins, He is faithful and just to forgive us our sins and to cleanse us from all unrighteousness" (1 John 1:9).

## REFLECTING ON THE TEXT

5)   What are some examples of idolatry that you see in the world today?

_____

_____

_____

_____

_____

_____

_____

6)   What are some of the consequences of idolatry present in our world? When have you experienced or had to grapple with those consequences?

_____

_____

_____

_____

_____

_____

_____

7) How do the idols of this world still tempt your heart? What steps can you take to remove those temptations from your life?

_____

_____

_____

_____

_____

8) Imagine you had a friend or loved one who desired to repent from idolatry. How would you lead that person through that process of repentance?

_____

_____

_____

_____

_____

## PERSONAL RESPONSE

9) What do you find are the drives, desires, or temptations that are most dangerous in terms of pushing you toward spiritual unfaithfulness?

_____

_____

_____

_____

_____

_____

10) What might it look like to direct those drives, desires, or temptations toward God? (What might it look like to seek fulfillment from God instead of something else?)

_____

_____

_____

_____

_____

# 9

# ADULTEROUS ISRAEL IN REBELLION
## Hosea 6:4–8:14

## DRAWING NEAR

Think back to a time when you confronted (or attempted to confront) someone who had wronged you. What did you do well in that exchange? What might you do differently?

-------------------------------------------------------------------------------

-------------------------------------------------------------------------------

-------------------------------------------------------------------------------

-------------------------------------------------------------------------------

## THE CONTEXT

As we have seen, chapters 1–3 of Hosea are unique in that God used the relationship between Hosea and the unfaithful Gomer as an illustration of His relationship with the unfaithful Israel. As we move into Hosea's descriptions of God's charges against Israel (4:1–10), the idolatry of Israel (4:11–19), God's impending judgment on Israel and Judah (5:1–15), and a call for repentance (6:1–3), the text begins to feel similar to the writings of other prophets.

Hosea has employed strong language and compelling imagery to highlight Israel's continuing rebellion against God while at the same time revealing the Lord's declaration that consequences were imminent in the form of captivity and exile at the hands of a foreign power (specifically Assyria). Hosea will continue these themes in chapters 6–8. In chapter 6, the prophet clarifies what God desires within the covenantal relationship. He states that the Lord is not satisfied by meaningless sacrifices or ceremonies but desires mercy and genuine knowledge of Himself. In other words, God wanted the Israelites to know Him and reflect His character.

In chapter 7, Hosea will continue to highlight the different ways that the Israelites had violated the covenant with God. Specifically, Hosea will call out the nation's continued attempts to seek assistance from foreign powers (like Egypt and Assyria) rather than returning to the Lord. In chapter 8, the prophet will go on to identify the specifics of Israel's apostasy—including their sin of pushing the southern kingdom of Judah toward the same wicked practices.

## Keys to the Text
Read Hosea 6:4–8:14, noting the key words and phrases indicated below.

> IMPENITENCE OF ISRAEL: *Because Israel's commitment to the Lord was fleeting and superficial, He had to send prophets with stern words, calling for a covenantal loyalty befitting a marriage relationship. But they violated the marriage vows.*

6:6. I DESIRE MERCY . . . NOT SACRIFICE: See 1 Samuel 15:22; Psalm 51:16–17; Matthew 9:13; 12:7.

7. COVENANT: A reference to the Mosaic covenant (see Hosea 8:1; Exodus 19:5–6).

8. GILEAD: See Hosea 12:11. A region located east of the Jordan River and north of the Jabbok. Most likely, the city of Ramoth Gilead is in view.

9. SHECHEM: This city is located forty miles north of Jerusalem in the central hill country, near Mount Ebal and Mount Gerizim. It was one of the forty-eight Levitical cities (see Joshua 20:7) and was the first capital of the northern kingdom (see 1 Kings 12:25).

11. ALSO, O JUDAH: Lest Judah feel smug at her neighbor's demise, the prophet reminds them that they have a day of reckoning also awaiting them (see Jeremiah 51:13; Joel 2:1–3).

7:1. SAMARIA: As the capital, Samaria represents the northern kingdom.

4–7. AN OVEN . . . AN OVEN . . . AN OVEN: The civil leaders' evil lust burned so passionately all night that the prophet repeatedly described it like a consuming oven (see verses 4, 6, 7)—so hot that the baker could forgo stirring the fire during the entire night and still have adequate heat for baking the next morning.

**7. ALL THEIR KINGS HAVE FALLEN:** Four of Israel's final six kings (Zechariah, Shallum, Pekahiah, and Pekah) were murdered by usurpers. See 2 Kings 15:8–16, 23–31.

**8–9. EPHRAIM HAS MIXED HIMSELF:** At Israel's invitation, foreign nations made debilitating inroads into her national and religious life. This intrusion was making her like "a cake unturned," burned on one side and raw on the other. Payment for this foreign assistance was "devouring her strength" and making her old and feeble without noticing it.

**10. THE PRIDE OF ISRAEL:** See note on Hosea 5:5.

> *FUTILE RELIANCE ON THE NATIONS: Like a dove, reputed to lack good sense (see Matthew 10:16), so Israel had sought assistance from Egypt and Assyria rather than from the Lord, and they would ultimately trap her.*

**13. REDEEMED THEM:** God had redeemed them from Egypt and their other enemies.

**14. WAILED UPON THEIR BEDS . . . ASSEMBLE TOGETHER:** The former phrase may speak of appeals to pagan fertility gods upon beds of sacred prostitution, while the latter, most likely, harkens to Elijah's encounter with the prophets of Baal on Mt. Carmel (see 1 Kings 18:28), based on an alternative translation of "gash themselves."

**8:1. SET THE TRUMPET:** To sound the alarm, for the divine conqueror approaches.

**LIKE AN EAGLE:** Literally a "vulture." Assyria was ready to descend quickly upon Israel to devour her (see Deuteronomy 28:49).

**TRANSGRESSED MY COVENANT:** See note on Hosea 6:7.

**2. WE KNOW YOU:** Israel's syncretistic and false worship, wherein she practiced idolatry while in vain crying out to God.

**4. KINGS . . . IDOLS:** The best human effort without God's true involvement is destined to fail.

**5–6. YOUR CALF IS REJECTED:** Calf worship was the national religion of the northern kingdom (see 1 Kings 12:25–33). This kind of worship had been rejected by God ever since it first appeared (see Exodus 32:1–35).

**7. SOW THE WIND . . . WHIRLWIND:** This indicates the escalating futility and uselessness of all their false religion.

9. THEY HAVE GONE UP TO ASSYRIA: As the context notes, this is not a reference to Israel's captivity but to the alliance she made with Assyria (see Hosea 7:11–12). "Like a wild donkey," Israel has stubbornly pursued foreign assistance rather than depending on the Lord.

11–12. I HAVE WRITTEN: Israel had been duly warned; she was without excuse (see Hosea 6:7; 8:1).

13. SHALL RETURN TO EGYPT: Recalling the place of Israel's former bondage, Hosea reminds the Israelites that Assyria will be their future "Egypt" (see Hosea 9:3; 11:5; Deuteronomy 28:68). A few Judean refugees actually did go to Egypt (see 2 Kings 25:26). Isaiah used "Sodom" in a similar representative fashion (see Isaiah 1:9–10).

14. JUDAH . . . FORTIFIED CITIES: Though less idolatrous than Israel, Judah (see note on Hosea 5:5) showed lack of faith in God by trusting more in fortifications. Instead of drawing near to God, Judah multiplied human defenses (see Isaiah 22:8; Jeremiah 5:17). All of these efforts to trust more in human means than to depend wholly on God are doomed to failure.

## UNLEASHING THE TEXT

1) How does God describe His people's unfaithfulness in Hosea 6:4–11?

_____

_____

_____

_____

_____

_____

_____

2) What can we learn from these chapters about what the Israelites valued and pursued? What was important to them?

_____

_____

_____

_____

_____

_____

_____

3) What can we learn from these chapters about what God expects His people to value and pursue? What does God consider to be important?

_____

_____

_____

_____

_____

_____

4) According to Hosea 7:11–16, why was it wrong or inappropriate for Israel to seek assistance from neighboring nations such as Egypt and Assyria?

_____

_____

_____

_____

_____

## Exploring the Meaning

***God desires connection with His people.*** One of the main consequences of Israel's idolatry and unfaithfulness was that the people became separated from God. This separation existed on a relational level. Whereas Adam walked with God in the cool of the day and Moses spoke to the Lord "face to face, as a man speaks to his friend" (Exodus 33:11), the Israelites had lost their fellowship with the Father. Why didn't the Israelites recognize their loss? Because they had substituted relational connection with religious practice. They continued observing the feasts, Sabbaths, sacrifices, and ceremonies prescribed in the Levitical law, yet their observation of that law remained at the surface. It was purely behavioral rather than relational. Through Hosea, God lamented that loss, telling the Israelites, "For I desire mercy and not sacrifice, and the knowledge of God more than burnt offerings" (6:6). The same is true today. God is not interested in church attendance or daily devotions as a replacement for genuine connection with Him. Instead, He seeks our hearts. As Jesus told His disciples, "No longer do I call you servants, for a servant does not know what his master is doing; but I have called you friends, for all things that I heard from My Father I have made known to you" (John 15:15).

***God desires obedience from His people.*** God seeks a relational connection with His people. This was true for the nation of Israel, and it remains true for disciples of Christ today. Through the death and resurrection of Jesus, we can know God even as we are known by Him. Still, the truth remains that God is our King in addition to our friend. He is our heavenly Father, and just like earthly fathers, He has made obedience a significant element in our relationship with Him. He desires us not only to know Him but also to obey His commands and reflect His values. God took great pains in highlighting the ways the Israelites had failed in this aspect of their relationship with God, concluding, "They do not consider in their hearts that I remember all their wickedness; now their own deeds have surrounded them; they are before My face" (7:2). It should be noted that Jesus also affirmed the connection between loving God and obeying God when He said, "You are My friends if you do whatever I command you" (John 15:14).

***God desires to bless His people.*** As part of God's relational connection with the Israelites, He desired to know His people, to receive obedience from His people, and also to be a source of blessing in their lives. God is by nature a Savior, and He actively desires to act on behalf of those He loves. Unfortunately, the Israelites had lost sight of this aspect of God's nature. Historically, they did not recognize the significance of everything God had done for their ancestors—for Abraham, Isaac, Jacob, Moses, Joshua, David, and others. Therefore, the Israelites of Hosea's day sought alliances with other nations as the solution for their temporary troubles. "Ephraim also is like a silly dove, without sense," wrote Hosea. "They call to Egypt, they go to Assyria" (7:11). This failure to seek God's protection and power was another evidence for and symptom of their spiritual unfaithfulness. They had lost faith in God's goodness and sovereignty. Likewise, we demonstrate lack of faith in God when we seek to overcome difficulties through our own resources rather than turning to Him for blessing, provision, and rescue.

## REFLECTING ON THE TEXT

5) What does it mean to demonstrate "knowledge of God"? What does it look like on a practical level to know Him?

_____

_____

_____

_____

6) What are some ways your relationship with God has grown and changed over the course of your spiritual life?

_____

_____

_____

_____

_____

_____

7) How can modern believers recognize when they are failing to obey God in specific areas? What steps can they take to discover their own disobedience?

_____

_____

_____

_____

_____

8) What are some possible reasons why we often view God as a last resort rather than a first option when we are in trouble or have a need?

_____

_____

_____

_____

_____

## PERSONAL RESPONSE

9) How are you planning to grow in your relationship with God over the coming year? What steps will you take to know Him better?

_____

_____

_____

_____

_____

10) Where are you in danger of disobeying God right now? What commands has He placed upon you that you have failed to obey?

_____

_____

_____

_____

_____

_____

_____

_____

# 10

# ADULTEROUS ISRAEL PUT AWAY

*Hosea 9:1 10:15*

## DRAWING NEAR

What are some things that you like most about your current home? What about your community?

_____

_____

_____

_____

_____

_____

_____

_____

## THE CONTEXT

Throughout the book of Hosea, the prophet has made hints and references toward Israel's future defeat at the hands of the Assyrians. That defeat would involve not only military slaughter and death but also captivity. The people would be removed from their covenantal home—the Promised Land—and relocated to foreign soil. This was an especially difficult consequence for the Israelites to imagine in light of their history.

Even so, Hosea made it clear that exile was a certainly. As we move into chapter 9, the prophet offers a more detailed look at what God's people would experience after being removed from their home: they would lose their joy, their

land, their spiritual discernment, their birth rate (ability to maintain a population), and their connection with God.

In chapter 10, the prophet continues the same theme. In spite of Israel's current prosperity (including plenty of food and supplies), their future was sealed
as a time of deprivation and distress. Israel's kings would be cut off, the people
would eat the fruit of their own wickedness, and the nation would be separated
from God's covenantal blessings.

## KEYS TO THE TEXT

Read Hosea 9:1–10:15, noting the key words and phrases indicated below.

> JUDGMENTS OF ISRAEL'S SIN: *Hosea enumerates the five features*
> *of the Lord's banishment of Israel to Assyria: (1) loss of joy,*
> *(2) exile, (3) loss of spiritual discernment, (4) declining birth rate,*
> *and (5) abandonment by God.*

9:1–2. THRESHING FLOOR . . . WINEPRESS: These were the very places where
sacred prostitution took place in an attempt to cause Baal to bring prosperity.
Instead, God brought poverty on them.

3. THE LORD'S LAND. See Leviticus 25:23.

EGYPT: See note on Hosea 8:13 (see also 11:5).

4. BREAD OF MOURNERS: Food eaten on the occasion of mourning was considered unclean, defiling anyone who ate it (see Deuteronomy 26:12–15).

6. MEMPHIS: An ancient capital of Egypt known for its tombs and pyramids.
This is used figuratively of Assyria, which would capture Samaria in 722 BC.
According to Assyrian records, 27,290 inhabitants of Israel were deported to distant locations. The relocation of populations was characteristic of Assyrian policy
during that era. The Israelites were resettled in the upper Tigris-Euphrates Valley
and never returned to the Promised Land (see 2 Kings 17:6–23).

7–8. PROPHET IS A FOOL . . . SPIRITUAL MAN IS INSANE: The true prophets
were God's inspired messengers and watchmen (see Ezekiel 3:17; 33:1–7), yet
Israel considered them fools and madmen. Thus, the nation was ensnared by the
words of the prophets because she chose to ignore the true words of warning.

9. GIBEAH: See Hosea 10:9. Israel's sin is likened to the gross evil of the men
of Gibeah, a reference to their heinous rape of the concubine (see Judges 19:22–
25), an infamous and unforgettable crime (see Judges 19:30).

10. GRAPES IN THE WILDERNESS: A rare and refreshing find (see Deuteronomy 32:10).

BAAL PEOR: Prior to entering the Promised Land, Israel fell into the idolatrous worship of Baal at Baal Peor (see Numbers 25:3–18). God killed 24,000 because of their immorality and false worship (see Numbers 25:9).

11–14. NO BIRTH, NO PREGNANCY . . . NO CONCEPTION: Reminiscent of the imprecatory psalms, Hosea prayed that God's blessing would be withdrawn, in the figure of withholding children, the ultimate earthly blessing.

13. TYRE: A prosperous Mediterranean coastal town south of Sidon. Just as Tyre will be severely judged (see Isaiah 13; Ezekiel 26–28), so will Israel.

15. GILGAL: As a center of idol worship (see note on Hosea 4:15), the place was representative of Israel's spiritual adultery; therefore, God had rejected them from intimate fellowship.

17. WANDERERS: God promised global dispersion for disobedience (see Leviticus 26:33; Deuteronomy 28:64–65). However, one day yet future, God will regather His covenant people back to their land (see Deuteronomy 30:3–4; Isaiah 11:12; Jeremiah 30:3; Ezekiel 37:21–22; Amos 9:14; Zephaniah 3:19–20; Zechariah 8:7–8).

> ISRAEL'S SIN AND CAPTIVITY: *Since Israel desired to be yoked with false deities and foreign kings, the Lord would really put them in a yoke of exile to Assyria.*

10:1. BRINGS FORTH FRUIT FOR HIMSELF: Agricultural prosperity had resulted in spiritual corruption (see Ezekiel 16:10–19).

2. BREAK DOWN THEIR ALTARS: Because Israel was no longer uniquely loyal to the Lord, He would destroy their false worship.

3–4. WE HAVE NO KING: The last five kings of Israel were usurpers. Impotent and unworthy of respect, they were incapable of enforcing the laws of the land.

5. THE CALF OF BETH AVEN: See notes on Hosea 4:15; 8:5.

6. KING JAREB: See note on Hosea 5:13.

8. AVEN: See notes on Hosea 4:15; 5:8.

COVER US . . . FALL ON US: The captivity would be so severe that the people would pray for the mountains and hills to fall on them, similar to the last days (see Luke 23:30; Revelation 6:16).

9. DAYS OF GIBEAH: See note on Hosea 9:9.

10. TWO TRANSGRESSIONS: Israel would receive a double portion of judgment for her iniquity (see Isaiah 40:2; Jeremiah 16:18).

11. A TRAINED HEIFER THAT LOVES TO THRESH GRAIN: This was a far easier work than plowing, since cattle were not bound together under a yoke but tread on the grain singly and were free to eat some of it, as the law required that they be unmuzzled (see Deuteronomy 25:4; 1 Corinthians 9:9).

14. SHALMAN PLUNDERED BETH ARBEL: Shalman was probably Shalmaneser V, king of Assyria (727–722 BC), who played a role in Israel's demise (see 2 Kings 17:3–6). Although the location of Beth Arbel is uncertain, the memory of the heinous crimes committed there was vividly etched into their minds.

15. BETHEL: See notes on Hosea 4:15; 5:8. The chief sanctuary of Israel (see Amos 7:13) and a center of idolatry (see 1 Kings 12:25–33; 2 Kings 10:29).

KING OF ISRAEL: Hoshea, who lived c. 732–722 BC, was the last king of Israel (see 2 Kings 17:1–6).

## UNLEASHING THE TEXT

1) What does Amos 9:7–9 reveal about how God's prophets were treated at this time in Israel's history? What does this say about the people's spiritual condition?

_____

_____

_____

_____

2) What do the images of "grapes in the wilderness" and "firstfruits on the fig tree" (9:10) reveal about how God had blessed His people?

_____

_____

_____

_____

3) What does God say the Israelites had done in response to receiving those blessings? According to 9:11–16, what would the consequences be for their actions?

_____

_____

_____

_____

4)   What spiritual principle does Hosea emphasize in 10:12–13?

_____

_____

_____

_____

_____

_____

_____

## EXPLORING THE MEANING

***We cannot ignore God's warnings.*** Hosea (and other prophets) told the Israelites that they had reaped God's judgment because of their idolatry. But what were the root causes that led them away from their covenantal relationship with God and left them seeking satisfaction through false gods? In other words, how did they arrive at such a dangerous precipice? One answer is that they ignored God's warnings—specifically, what God had declared through His prophets. According to Hosea, the people had rejected God's messengers, saying, "The prophet is a fool, the spiritual man is insane" (9:7). When the prophets spoke truth in a way the people found offensive, they rejected those prophets' messages by labeling them as untrustworthy and even ridiculous. As a result, "The days of punishment have come; the days of recompense have come. Israel knows!" (verse 7). Jesus warned His disciples they would encounter a similar obstacle: "Now brother will deliver up brother to death, and a father his child; and children will rise up against parents and cause them to be put to death. And you will be hated by all for My name's sake" (Matthew 10:21–22). Standing for God often means facing rejection from men.

***We must avoid ungodly leaders.*** Not only did the Israelites reject the prophets whom God sent to steer them back in the right direction, but they also embraced leaders who actively sought to drive Israel deeper into idolatry. The Israelites openly followed and approved of wicked leaders. In chapter 7, Hosea declared of Israel, "All their kings have fallen. None among them calls upon Me" (verse 7). This reference to "all their kings" is significant because of the political turmoil that existed in Israel's last decades. As noted, Israel had no fewer than six kings during its final thirty years, and four of those rulers were murdered by usurpers. So Israel had no political stability. Worse, the kings who did rule were not righteous men. Instead, they actively pushed the nation further into idolatry and foreign gods. In Hosea's words, "All their princes are rebellious" (9:15). It seems the people did eventually tire of their wicked leaders. "For now they say, 'We have no king, because we did not fear the LORD,' " wrote Hosea. "And as for a king, what would he do for us?" (10:3). The government was incapable of enforcing God's law because the Israelites had put their faith in evil leaders—and those leaders led them astray.

*We must value pleasing God over our own pleasure.* A third reason for the Israelites' unfaithfulness toward God was their singular focus on their own comfort and pleasure. "You have made love for hire on every threshing floor," Hosea said to them, referring also to the "winepress" (9:1)—references to pagan rituals involving sacred prostitution. God's people had joined with temple prostitutes for pleasure and to seek a fruitful harvest. As a reminder, Hosea began prophesying during the reign of Jeroboam II, which was a relatively prosperous period in Israel's history. That agricultural boon resulted in spiritual corruption: "Israel empties his vine; he brings forth fruit for himself. According to the multitude of his fruit he has increased the altars; according to the bounty of his land they have embellished his sacred pillars" (10:1). This is an important principle for modern disciples of Jesus; namely, that worldly prosperity is a danger to spiritual maturity. Because we live in a time and place that is filled with intense pressure to pursue pleasure, we often fail to realize how much time and attention we are funneling toward our own comfort—and away from our worship of and devotion to our Lord.

## REFLECTING ON THE TEXT

5) What are some ways God warns and directs His people today? How have you experienced those warnings?

_____

_____

_____

_____

_____

_____

_____

6) We live in a culture that does not always value spiritual maturity in its leaders. How, then, should Christians approach the political process on local and national levels?

_____

_____

_____

_____

_____

7) What does the culture emphasize (and even insist on) concerning the pursuit of pleasure as a necessary element of life?

_____

_____

_____

_____

_____

8) How have you observed the connection between your own personal comfort and your devotion to Christ?

_____

_____

_____

_____

## PERSONAL RESPONSE

9) To what degree is your spiritual life based on following human leaders rather than knowing and interacting with Jesus?

_____

_____

_____

_____

10) What is one step you can take this week to actively deny or step away from the pursuit of comfort and pleasure?

_____

_____

_____

_____

_____

_____

_____

# 11

## ADULTEROUS ISRAEL RESTORED
### Hosea 11:1–14:9

## DRAWING NEAR
Why is reconciliation and forgiveness so refreshing?

_____

_____

_____

_____

_____

_____

_____

_____

_____

_____

## THE CONTEXT
We do not always think of Scripture in terms of emotional impact, but there is no
doubt the Bible is emotionally rich. The Psalms, in particular, capture a range
of emotions: loneliness (see Psalm 25:16), sorrow (see 31:10), grief (see 6:7), anger
(see 4:4), joy (see 4:7), hope (see 33:22), and others. The Song of Solomon is a love
song filled with emotion that exalts the purity of marital affection and romance.
There are also emotionally charged stories such as Jesus being moved with compassion over the masses (see Matthew 14:14), overturning the tables of the money-
changers (see Mark 11:15), and weeping at the death of Lazarus (see John 11:35).

Hosea 11 is perhaps one of the most deeply emotional moments in Scripture. Surprisingly, it is God who expresses the emotions—albeit as an anthropopathism. The Lord recounts through Hosea how He loved Israel as "a child" and called them "out of Egypt" (Hosea 11:1), recalling the events of the Exodus when Moses led the people of Israel out of Egypt. God taught Israel "to walk," led them "by their arms," and "stooped and fed them" (Hosea 11:3–4). These are the tender words of a loving heavenly Father who longs for His people to return to Him.

Hosea 12 and 13 return to the primary theme of Israel's unfaithfulness, contrasting the people with Jacob the patriarch, who sought the Lord with diligence. Finally, the prophet concludes in Hosea 14 by looking forward to the restoration of Israel during the Millennial kingdom and exhorting his readers to choose obedience and faithfulness over folly.

## KEYS TO THE TEXT

Read Hosea 11:1–14:9, noting the key words and phrases indicated below.

> GOD'S CONTINUING LOVE FOR ISRAEL: *In tender words reminiscent*
> *of the Exodus from Egypt (see Exodus 4:22–23), the Lord reassures*
> *Israel of His intense love for her.*

11:1. OUT OF EGYPT I CALLED MY SON: God's compassion for Israel was aroused in this passage (see Isaiah 12:1; 40:1, 2; 49:13; Jeremiah 31:10–14; Zechariah 1:12–17). See Matthew 2:15 for Matthew's analogical use of this verse in relationship to Jesus Christ.

3–4. I TAUGHT EPHRAIM TO WALK: The Lord's endearing word pictures in these verses are reflected in Ezekiel's touching descriptions of Israel's early years (see Ezekiel 16:1–14).

5. SHALL NOT RETURN TO . . . EGYPT: See note on Hosea 8:13.

5–7. THEY REFUSED TO REPENT: In spite of God's tender care, Israel was ungrateful, deserving punishment (see Romans 1:21).

7. BACKSLIDING: This term is often used by the prophets (see Isaiah 57:17; Jeremiah 3:6, 8, 11–14, 22; 8:5; 31:22; 49:4; Hosea 14:4) of apostate unbelievers (see also Proverbs 14:14).

8. ADMAH . . . ZEBOIIM: Because of the Lord's great love for Ephraim, it was painful to punish her as He did these two cities, which were destroyed with Sodom and Gomorrah (see Genesis 10:19; 19:23–25; Deuteronomy 29:23).

9. I WILL NOT AGAIN DESTROY EPHRAIM: The destruction referred to that inflicted by the Assyrian king Tiglath-Pileser, who deprived Israel of Gilead, Galilee, and Naphtali (see 2 Kings 15:29). Ultimately, it referred to the promise that after the long dispersion, God would, in mercy, restore His people in the kingdom, never to be destroyed again. See note on Hosea 9:17.

10. WILL ROAR LIKE A LION: Although the Lord would, as a lion, roar against Israel in judgment (see Hosea 5:14; 13:7), He would also roar for the purpose of calling, protecting, and blessing her (see Joel 3:16).

FROM THE WEST: Returns from Assyrian and Babylonian captivities were from the east. This undoubtedly has reference to Jesus' return at the Second Advent to set up the Millennial kingdom (see Isaiah 11:11–12), when He calls Israel from their worldwide dispersion and reverses the judgment of Hosea 9:17.

11. EGYPT . . . ASSYRIA: See note on Hosea 8:13.

12. STILL WALKS WITH GOD: See note on Hosea 5:5. In keeping with the other mentions of Judah by Hosea, this phrase is better translated "is unruly against God" (see 12:2).

> ISRAEL'S SINS REBUKED BY GOD: *Israel's attempted alliances*
> *with heathen neighbors were of no worth. This prophecy was*
> *delivered at about the time of Israel's seeking aid from the*
> *Assyrian and Egyptian kings (see 2 Kings 17:1–4).*

12:2. JUDAH: See note on Hosea 5:5.

JACOB: Used interchangeably with "Israel" (see Hosea 10:11; Genesis 32:28).

3–6. BROTHER . . . HEEL . . .STRUGGLED . . . ANGEL: This refers to the events of Jacob's birth (see Genesis 25:22–28) and his struggle with the Angel of the Lord, who is also identified as God (see 32:22–32). Hosea exhorted the people to follow their father Jacob's persevering prayerfulness, which brought God's favor on him. As God is unchanging, He would show the same favor to Jacob's posterity if, like him, they truly sought God.

4. BETHEL: See Genesis 28:10–22; 31:13; 35:9–15.

5. LORD . . . MEMORABLE NAME: In Exodus 3:14, the Lord told Moses, "I AM WHO I AM." This name for God points to His self-existence and eternality; it denotes "I am the One who is/will be." The consonants from the Hebrew word *Yhwh*, combined with the vowels from the divine name *Adonai* (Master or Lord), gave rise to the name "Jehovah" in English. Since the name Yahweh was considered

so sacred it should not be pronounced, the Massoretes inserted the vowels from Adonai to remind themselves to pronounce it when reading instead of saying Yahweh. This combination of consonants is known as the "tetragrammaton."

7–8. CANAANITE: Because the Canaanites were known as traders, the word came to be used synonymously with "merchant" (see Ezekiel 16:29; 17:4; Zephaniah 1:11). Though she denied it (verse 8), Israel had become materialistic, filled with greed, and fond of dishonest gain.

9. DWELL IN TENTS: At the annual Feast of Tabernacles, also called the Feast of Booths (see Numbers 29:12–38), Israel lived in tents to commemorate her forty years of wilderness wanderings. In captivity, she would be forced to live in tents permanently.

10. I HAVE ALSO SPOKEN: Here is an aggravation of their guilt, that it was not through ignorance that they sinned, but in defiance of God's revealed Word (see Amos 3:8).

11. GILEAD: See note on Hosea 6:8.

GILGAL: See notes on Hosea 4:15; 9:15. Gilgal means "a heap of stones," so this is a play on words.

HEAPS IN THE FURROWS: As gathered and piled stones would dot a farmer's field, so Israel multiplied her idolatrous stone altars across the land.

12–14. JACOB FLED . . . BROUGHT ISRAEL OUT OF EGYPT: The reference to Jacob's wanderings to Syria (see Genesis 28:1–5; 29:1–30) and Israel's escape from Egypt by Moses's hand (see Exodus 12–15) should cause Ephraim to confess her pride, recognize her humble origins, and acknowledge that only by God's gracious power were they made and preserved as a nation.

13:1. TREMBLING: When Ephraim, the most powerful tribe (see Genesis 48:17–20), spoke early in Israel's history, it was with authority and produced fear.

BAAL: See note on Hosea 2:8.

HE DIED: Because of his sins and in spite of being feared, Ephraim died spiritually, and now nationally.

2. KISS THE CALVES: An act of their ridiculous devotion to their idols (see 1 Kings 19:18).

3. CLOUD . . . DEW . . . CHAFF . . . SMOKE: These four similes vividly describe the spiritual futility, vanity, emptiness, and bankruptcy of idolatry.

4–6. I AM THE LORD YOUR GOD: Having entered into a marriage covenant with the Lord, Israel was to remain faithful to Him alone (see Exodus 20:2–3), yet she forgot Him.

4. NO GOD BUT ME: All false gods stand in opposition to the true God, and the worship of them is incompatible with the worship of Yahweh. Israel had blatantly violated the first two commandments of the Torah.

NO SAVIOR BESIDES ME: See Isaiah 43:11. God is by nature a Savior, both temporally and eternally. God delivered Israel from Egypt and will deliver her from Babylon and all future exiles, as well as bring her to spiritual salvation (see Zechariah 12:10–13:1; Romans 11:25–27).

5. WILDERNESS . . . DROUGHT. God cared for the nation's needs during their wilderness wanderings, providing water (see Exodus 17:1–7) and food (see Numbers 16).

6. FILLED: God brought the people into a land of milk and honey (see Exodus 3:8; Deuteronomy 6:3), but they turned their worship to other gods (see Deuteronomy 31:20), as Moses prophesied.

7–8. LION . . . LEOPARD . . . BEAR: These animals are all native to Israel. Her Protector would now become to her as a wild beast, tearing and devouring in judgment because of Israel's spiritual promiscuity (see Leviticus 26:21, 22; Deuteronomy 32:24; Ezekiel 14:21).

9. DESTROYED . . . HELP: The one who helped the Israelites (see Hosea 13:4) is the one who will destroy them in judgment (see verse 8).

10. YOUR KING: This is better translated, "Where is your king?" This is an indictment of Israel for not recognizing the Lord as their true king (see 1 Samuel 10:17–19).

11. I GAVE YOU A KING: This probably spans the time from Israel's first king, Saul, c. 1011 BC (see 1 Samuel 15:26), to Israel's last king, Hoshea, 722 BC (see 2 Kings 17:7–18).

12. BOUND UP . . . STORED UP: Israel's sins are all well documented and safely preserved for the day of reckoning (see Hosea 7:2; Deuteronomy 32:34–35; Job 14:17).

13. WHERE CHILDREN ARE BORN: This refers to the birth canal. Using this figure of giving birth, the Lord compares Ephraim to an unwise child, unwilling to move through to birth. By long deferring a "new birth" with repentance, the nation was like a child remaining in the canal dangerously long and risking death (see 2 Kings 19:3; Isaiah 37:3; 66:9).

14. I WILL RANSOM THEM: Placing the strong affirmation of deliverance so abruptly after a denunciation intensified the wonder of God's unrequited love (see Hosea 11:8–9; Leviticus 26:44). This can apply to God's restoration of Israel

from Assyria and in future times from all the lands of the dispersion, preserving them and bringing them back to their land for the kingdom of Messiah (see Ezekiel 37). It also speaks of the time of personal resurrection, as in Daniel 12:2–3. Repentant Israelites will be restored to the land and even raised from death to glory. Paul uses this text in 1 Corinthians 15:55 (quoting the LXX) to celebrate the future resurrection of the church. The Messiah's great victory over death and the grave is the firstfruits of the full harvest to come, when all believers will likewise experience the power of His resurrection.

15. EAST WIND: This refers to Assyria. See Hosea 12:1.

16. SAMARIA: See note on Hosea 7:1.

FALL . . . DASHED . . . RIPPED: These shocking atrocities were in keeping with brutalities characteristic of the Assyrians (see 2 Kings 17:5; Isaiah 13:6; Amos 1:13; Nahum 3:10).

> ISRAEL RESTORED AT LAST: *Hosea ends with an invitation for Israel to return to God, bringing words of repentance accompanied with obedience, repaying God's gracious acceptance of them with genuine "sacrifices of our lips" (Hosea 14:2).*

14:1. OUR LIPS: God condemns lip service worship (see Isaiah 29:13; Matthew 15:8).

3. FATHERLESS: Dependence on other nations, military might, and idols left Israel as though an orphan. God repeatedly demanded mercy for the orphan (see Exodus 22:22; Deuteronomy 10:18); consequently, Israel could expect to receive His compassion (see Luke 15:17–20).

4–8. I WILL HEAL: The ultimate fulfillment of these blessings must be millennial, since Israel has not, nor will not, repent in the manner of Hosea 14:2–3 until the end of the Great Tribulation (see Zechariah 12:10–13:1). The Lord's love is beautifully presented in metaphors taken from the morning dew, the lily, the cedars of Lebanon, the olive tree, grain, the grapevine, and the cypress tree.

4. BACKSLIDING: See note on Hosea 11:7.

7. THEIR SCENT . . . LIKE THE WINE OF LEBANON: Their scent (literally "remembrance") denotes worldwide fame and admiration.

8. YOUR FRUIT IS FOUND IN ME: The Lord, not idols, will care for Israel. He, not Israel, is the tree providing shelter and prosperity, the "green cypress tree" from whom her fruitfulness would come.

9. WISE . . . PRUDENT: Representative of the book's theme, Hosea's epilogue concludes the prophecy by presenting the reader with two ways of living, obediently or disobediently (see Deuteronomy 30:19–20; Psalm 1). He appeals to all readers to be wise, to choose the Lord's way, because His ways are right (see Psalm 107:43; Ecclesiastes 12:13–14).

## UNLEASHING THE TEXT

1) What do the images used in Hosea 11:1–4 reveal about God's disposition toward Israel?

_____

_____

_____

_____

2) What can we learn about Judah, the southern kingdom, from Hosea 11 and 12?

_____

_____

_____

_____

3) Hosea 13:7–8 describes God using the imagery of a lion, leopard, and bear. What do you learn about God's character based on those descriptions?

_____

_____

_____

_____

4) How would you describe Hosea's concluding message or exhortation in chapter 14? What did he want his readers to learn (and do) based on his prophecy?

_____

_____

_____

_____

## EXPLORING THE MEANING

***God's love for His children is tender.*** The word pictures and descriptions in Hosea 11 are stunning in their tenderness and compassion. God describes loving Israel as a child, even teaching Ephraim to walk. He speaks of healing and feeding His wayward son and of drawing His people forward with bands of love. Perhaps even more poignant is the grief God expresses regarding the necessity of Israel's destruction and captivity. The pain is evident as God cries out, "How can I give you up, Ephraim? How can I hand you over, Israel? How can I make you like Admah? How can I set you like Zeboiim? My heart churns within Me; My sympathy is stirred" (11:8). What these verses reveal is that God is by nature a Father. His Father-ness (or His Father's heart) is a vital part of His character and plays a major role in how He relates to His people. Notably, God did not choose to change or negate His plan for the Assyrians to conquer Israel and take the people into captivity—sin still required justice. Yet these verses reflect a more perfect version of every parent who knows their children must experience consequences and yet also desires to shield them from those consequences.

***God's love for His children is fierce.*** Near the end of Hosea 11, God describes Himself as a lion when dealing with His children: "When He roars, then His sons shall come trembling from the west; they shall come trembling like a bird from Egypt, like a dove from the land of Assyria" (verses 10–11). This aspect of God's love is authoritative—when He calls in power, His children will obey. In chapter 13, God uses similar imagery but with a different meaning: "So I will be to them like a lion; like a leopard by the road I will lurk; I will meet them like a bear deprived of her cubs; I will tear open their rib cage, and there I will devour them like a lion. The wild beast shall tear them" (verses 7–8). These verses are shocking in their violence, revealing the magnitude of grief and pain the Israelites would experience because of their continued rebellion. Yet even in the next verse, God affirms His fierce and faithful love for His people: "O Israel, you are destroyed, but your help is from Me. I will be your King" (verses 9–10). Once again, God serves as a loving Father by operating from seemingly opposite sides of the same coin. He is protective but also just—He helps even by harming. God operates as the perfect Father whose love for His children encompasses the full range of His character.

***God's love for His children is never ending.*** There are many instances in Hosea where God emphasizes the timeless nature of His love for the Israelites. As we have seen, He remembered His earliest encounters with Abraham and his descendants—what was history to the people of Israel was the living present to their heavenly Father. In a similar way, God often points forward to Israel's future—specifically, the time of restoration in Christ's Millennial Kingdom, when all wrongs will be made right and His covenantal relationship with Israel will be fully restored. This striking passage from Hosea's prophecy also provides a foreshadowing of the gospel and God's incredible gift of eternal life: "I will ransom them from the power of the grave; I will redeem them from death. O Death, I will be your plagues! O Grave, I will be your destruction!" (13:14). While God's love for Israel required punitive action during Hosea's day, His ultimate love for His people is unceasing and will result in unending joy for all of His children.

## REFLECTING ON THE TEXT

5)   How have you experienced God's love? What are the effects of His love?

_____

_____

_____

_____

_____

6)   When have you experienced God's love through the vehicle of discipline or a painful moment? How did that experience impact you?

_____

_____

_____

_____

_____

7)   What obstacles—including your own sins—still hinder you from experiencing the full spectrum of God's love?

_____

_____

_____

_____

_____

8) Look at Hosea's epilogue in 14:9. What does it look like for someone to "walk" correctly in light of the principles Hosea shared and the problems he exposed?

_____

_____

_____

_____

_____

_____

## PERSONAL RESPONSE

9) Consider the dynamic way Hosea depicts God's love for His children. How have you experienced these various aspects of your heavenly Father's love? Explain.

_____

_____

_____

_____

_____

_____

10) Where are you currently walking through difficulty or perhaps even discipline? What is one step you can take to embrace God's love within that situation?

_____

_____

_____

_____

_____

_____

# 12

# REVIEWING KEY PRINCIPLES

## DRAWING NEAR

What has most challenged you in this study of Jonah, Amos, and Hosea?

_____
_____
_____
_____
_____
_____
_____
_____
_____
_____
_____
_____
_____
_____
_____

## THE CONTEXT

On the surface, Jonah, Amos, and Hosea seem like three very different books in terms of literary style and subject matter. Yet below the surface, all three address the same dual theme of human faithlessness contrasted with the unfailing faithfulness of God.

Jonah was a prophet called by God to deliver a message of wrath as a vehicle of grace to a wicked people. Yet the prophet himself proved unfaithful, even as God remained steadfast by showing mercy first to Jonah in spite of his disobedience and then to the residents of the city of Nineveh. Amos and Hosea were faithful in delivering God's warning of impending doom, even as the recipients of that warning continued their rebellion against the God who set them apart and extended His love to them. Again, God remained faithful by carrying out His just discipline with the goal of restoration. In all these things, and in every way, God remained faithful.

Below you will find a few additional principles we explored during our study of Jonah, Amos, and Hosea. There are many more we do not have room to reiterate, so take some time to review the earlier studies—or better still, to meditate on the passages of Scripture we have covered. As you do, ask the Holy Spirit to give you wisdom and insight into His Word.

## EXPLORING THE MEANING

*God has sovereign power to bring about His will.* God designed human beings with the ability to choose and make decisions, so we can understand the reality of God's will in this world in a small way. Like our Creator, we have the ability to develop preferences, plans, desires, and designs (see Proverbs 16:9). But this is where the similarities end, for the Bible also reveals that God's thoughts and His ways are higher than our own (see Isaiah 55:8–9). Furthermore, as we see in Jonah 1, God has the perfect ability to bring about His will through His sovereign power. God not only makes plans, but He also makes them happen. He possesses the resources to accomplish whatever He desires—which can include sovereignly arranging "a great wind," controlling the outcome of sailors casting lots, and miraculously providing a "great fish" to swallow His servant. Notice that God's sovereignty is not limited by the will of human beings. In fact, God predestined to accomplish His purposes through the actions of men. Jonah desired to disobey God; that was his will, and he attempted to act on it. Yet God worked through the circumstances in Jonah's life so as to accomplish His sovereign plan.

*Our heavenly Father is a gracious and patient God.* As you read through Jonah, it's difficult to miss the similarities between the two commissions that God delivered to His prophet: "Now the word of the LORD came to Jonah the son of Amittai, saying, 'Arise, go to Nineveh, that great city, and cry out against it;

for their wickedness has come up before Me' " (1:1–2); "Now the word of the LORD came to Jonah the second time, saying, 'Arise, go to Nineveh, that great city, and preach to it the message that I tell you' " (3:1–2). Jonah's second chance was a tangible reflection of God's grace and patience. The prophet had already failed in following God's first command by attempting to run away from the Lord's will—something Jonah should have known to be impossible. Even so, God showed mercy to His prophet. God also showed mercy to the people of Nineveh, who were renowned for their wickedness. Jonah's declaration—"Yet forty days, and Nineveh shall be overthrown!" (3:4)—was not a bluff. The Assyrians were deserving of God's wrath, yet, due to His grace, God granted them salvation, which they did not deserve.

*God's judgments are always deserved.* Throughout history, cultures have told stories about false gods who were capricious in nature. These gods were petty, violent, and vengeful without cause and commonly carried out punishments that were undeserved. Even in Western culture today, there is a sense that God (or some version of a generic deity) delivers punishments in ways that are haphazard. But none of these attributes can be applied to the God of the Bible. Instead, He operates as a just Judge who carries out His judgments with fairness. We see this in Amos 1–2, where each of the judgments pronounced by the prophet makes it clear how a specific region or nation transgressed against God and earned His wrath. For instance, in pronouncing judgment against Ammon, God clearly reported its crime: "Because they ripped open the women with child in Gilead, that they might enlarge their territory" (1:13). Their brutality against the innocent brought consequences. In addition, each judgment in Amos 1–2 contains the rhetorical phrase, "for three transgressions . . . for four." This shows that God was not pronouncing judgment against isolated mistakes but for repeated transgressions.

*God hears the prayers of His people.* Amos spoke of two visions he received from the Lord in 7:1–6. In the first vision, he saw a swarm of locusts devastating the crops of Israel. In the second vision, Amos saw God calling for "conflict by fire" that "consumed" (verse 4) much of Israel's territory. Both times Amos received those visions, he responded by crying out to God and interceding on behalf of the people. He asked God to "forgive" and "cease" His judgments, and in both cases, he concluded his prayer with this supplication: "Oh, that Jacob may stand, for he is small!" (verses 2, 5). And in both cases, God responded by relenting from His wrath and stating, "It shall not be" (verse 3). What do we learn from these visions? First and foremost, that God hears the prayers of His people. As the apostle John wrote, "Now this is the confidence that we have in Him, that if we ask anything according to His will, He hears us" (1 John 5:14). God not only hears our prayers but also responds to them in accordance with His sovereign will.

***God can rebuild what seems lost.*** Amos's vision of God destroying the altar at Bethel offered a foreshadowing of the destruction on the horizon for the entire northern kingdom of Israel. The Assyrians not only destroyed Bethel in 722 BC but also put thousands of Israelites to the sword and carried the rest away into captivity. For those Israelites, it seemed that God's promises of a homeland for His people were lost beyond repair. Yet the final verses of Amos strike a more hopeful tone: "On that day I will raise up the tabernacle of David, which has fallen down, and repair its damages; I will raise up its ruins, and rebuild it as in the days of old" (9:11). No longer focused on the altar at Bethel, God instead spoke of "the tabernacle of David." This was a reference to God's promise in 2 Samuel 7 that He would build David a "house" that would stand forever. That house was David's dynasty, which culminated in the Messiah, Jesus Christ. As part of that promise, God also declared, "Moreover I will appoint a place for My people Israel, and will plant them, that they may dwell in a place of their own and move no more; nor shall the sons of wickedness oppress them anymore" (2 Samuel 7:10). This promise seemed lost for the people of Israel when Assyria invaded their land—and later for the people of Judah when Babylon destroyed Jerusalem. Yet the final verses of Amos point forward to the ultimate fulfillment of God's promises to His people: "'I will plant them in their land, and no longer shall they be pulled up from the land I have given them,' says the LORD your God" (9:15).

***We are called to be faithful to God.*** The marriage between Hosea and Gomer served as an illustration of the relationship between God and His people. But it is important to understand that Hosea's marriage was not a metaphor; he took Gomer as his wife, and the text seems to indicate that he desired her to be faithful to him—and to their children. In the same way that Hosea expected faithfulness from Gomer, so God expected faithfulness from the Israelites. The connection between God and His people was also not a metaphor. God had entered into a covenant with Abraham's descendants—similar to a marriage covenant—in which He said, "I will take you as My people, and I will be your God" (Exodus 6:7). Followers of Jesus are also expected to maintain a spiritually faithful relationship with God. In fact, the New Testament uses similar imagery of the church as Christ's "bride." As Paul wrote, "Husbands, love your wives, just as Christ also loved the church and gave Himself for her, that He might sanctify and cleanse her with the washing of water by the word" (Ephesians 5:25–26). The book of Revelation uses this same terminology, stating, "Let us be glad and rejoice and give Him glory, for the marriage of the Lamb has come, and His wife has made herself ready" (19:7).

*God desires connection with His people.* One of the main consequences of Israel's idolatry and unfaithfulness was that the people became separated from God. This separation existed on a relational level. Whereas Adam walked with God in the cool of the day and Moses spoke to the Lord "face to face, as a man speaks to his friend" (Exodus 33:11), the Israelites had lost their fellowship with the Father. Why didn't the Israelites recognize their loss? Because they had substituted relational connection with religious practice. They continued observing the feasts, Sabbaths, sacrifices, and ceremonies prescribed in the Levitical law, yet their observation of that law remained at the surface. It was purely behavioral rather than relational. Through Hosea, God lamented that loss, telling the Israelites, "For I desire mercy and not sacrifice, and the knowledge of God more than burnt offerings" (6:6). The same is true today. God is not interested in church attendance or daily devotions as a replacement for genuine connection with Him. Instead, He seeks our hearts. As Jesus told His disciples, "No longer do I call you servants, for a servant does not know what his master is doing; but I have called you friends, for all things that I heard from My Father I have made known to you" (John 15:15).

*We cannot ignore God's warnings.* Hosea (and other prophets) told the Israelites that they had reaped God's judgment because of their idolatry. But what were the root causes that led them away from their covenantal relationship with God and left them seeking satisfaction through false gods? In other words, how did they arrive at such a dangerous precipice? One answer is that they ignored God's warnings—specifically, what God had declared through His prophets. According to Hosea, the people had rejected God's messengers, saying, "The prophet is a fool, the spiritual man is insane" (9:7). When the prophets spoke truth in a way the people found offensive, they rejected those prophets' messages by labeling them as untrustworthy and even ridiculous. As a result, "The days of punishment have come; the days of recompense have come. Israel knows!" (verse 7). Jesus warned His disciples they would encounter a similar obstacle: "Now brother will deliver up brother to death, and a father his child; and children will rise up against parents and cause them to be put to death. And you will be hated by all for My name's sake" (Matthew 10:21–22). Standing for God often means facing rejection from men.

## UNLEASHING THE TEXT

1) What passages have encouraged you the most in this study? Why?

_____

_____

_____

_____

2) What has challenged you while reading the words of Jonah, Amos, or Hosea? Why did those things challenge you?

_____

_____

_____

_____

3) How has studying these prophets added to your understanding and your love of Christ?

_____

_____

_____

_____

4) How would you describe faithfulness and faithful love in history? In your life?

_____

_____

_____

_____

## PERSONAL RESPONSE

5) Have you repented of your sin and placed your faith in the finished work of Jesus Christ? Do you strive to put off sin and put on righteousness out of love for Him? Explain.

6) What sins have you been most convicted of during this study? What will you do to address these sins? What will that look like over time? Be specific.

7) What have you learned about God's nature and character throughout this study? How should that knowledge affect your everyday life?

8) In what areas do you hope to grow spiritually over the coming weeks and months? What steps will you need to take in order to achieve that growth?

If you would like to continue in your study of the Old Testament, read the next title in this series: *Micah, Zephaniah, Nahum, Habakkuk, Joel, and Obadiah.*

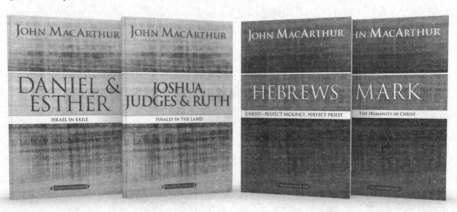

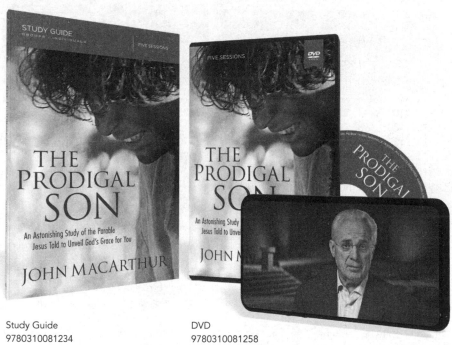

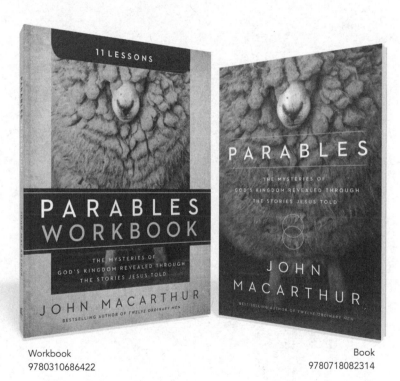